NEDWORLD

The complete guide to Ned life and living

KYLIE PILRIG & KEANU McGLINCHY

BLACK & WHITE PUBLISHING

First published 2005
by Black & White Publishing Ltd
99 Giles Street, Edinburgh, EH6 6BZ

ISBN 1 84502 058 8

A CIP catalogue record for this book is available
from the British Library.

Printed and bound by Nørhaven Paperback A/S

Contents

Acknowledgements

Kylie Diva Pilrig wants to thank everyone at Black & White Publishing – you're all fab, by the way; everyone at the Hilton NHS Hairmyres and Hilton NHS Monklands for getting Keanu out alive; B-B – thanx for all the support, BTW; Peter, as ever, and for the eleventh hour stuff; everyone at Waterstone's, Ottakar's, Borders and W H Smith and all the indi's out there – thank you for selling this book to pay for her new diddies and please don't ban it, by the way; Ellie and Tommy and Scoobie; Ron P for the blonde stuff; Mr P for 'dick-daft' and all the grub; Mikey and RP for the limericks; her ma and bro and Evie; Inez; Ros G, keep on fiddling; Boozy; Lornsk; Miss D – bling-bling, dahling; K&T; Cynth and team; TF and Ian; Wee Wobbs; FdotT; Carolski; Traceoochka; Sara H; hairdresser Ian at Curlers – the extensions are to pure die for; Chris; Simon B; gorgeous Lynnie Cleavage; Patti and Stud; Hels D; all her pals – thanks for the jokes; Jane – pure gold; Eleeseum and G – Hollywood look out!; Klepto F for the cover ideas and Sandra for the funeral contributions; Mrs A for getting him well AND, most of all, Keanu the Big Man, without whom . . .

Keanu wants to thank Vauxhall for giving the world the Corsa; Citroen for the Saxo and FIAT for the Punto. He also wishes to thank Saxosportsclub.com for all their help on his modifications.

Introduction

Welcome to Nedworld!

See us, man? We're Keanu and Kylie, cousins from Govan, and this publisher asked us to write a book about oor lives. We reckon we get a hard time just cos of the way we look, the way we drive, the way we talk and the way we act – and cos we have kids at a young age. But we don't live in a rat race, getting pure stressed about work and meeting deadlines – although writing this book has been more stressful than one of Keanu's court appearances.

We read in the *Record* the other day that Collins have just put us in their dictionary, man. We've pure made dictionaries famous cos now 'ned' is included as a real word and we could be worth twenty points on a Scrabble board. We hope you are not pure jealous of oor lives, man, cos, in this book, there are stories by us and some of oor mates about oor daily lives and oor families.

We hope you'll buy this book and, if you do, thank you, cos Kylie wants implants with her royalty money tae become a glamour model and Ah want tae get some new artwork along the side of ma Corsa. Ah used to acquire other people's cars but Ah saved up ma buroo money tae buy the Corsa and Ah'm pure loving being mobile.

QUALITY! We love you all. C U l8r.

Kylie ☺

KEANU
(too, by the way)

Keanu and Kylie

1

Ned Dating and Sex
by Keanu and Kylie

Haw, see me and Keanu? We started dating – no' each other though cos we're cousins and that would be pure gross – before books were invented, man. And we didn't need a book tae tell us what tae dae. Naw, man. We started at the back of the upstairs of the bus and continued from there, man. Ah moved on to the bus stop pretty early – about nine, man – but Keanu was a bit later. Mind you, boys are late starters, know what Ah mean?

Keanu used a graveyard, man. He used tae get together with his pals in there and then some girls came along, man, and, before you knew it, the stones didn't know what had hit them, by the way. His best pal, Crash, thought it was pure disrespectful but he pure changed his tune after he got his first graveyard lumber.

Keanu had a string of burds that pure idolised him cos he was a pure rebel. He stole loads of cars and attracts the girls cos he looks like Jensen Button with acne and pure pasty white skin, man. He used to cruise past the Spar and the McDonald's Drive Thru to pick up the burds – they totally loved it, man. Thank fuck he never got any of them pregnant – not for the want of trying, by the way.

Wish Ah could say the same. Ah was pure dick-daft as a wean. Ah had Britney when Ah was just turned twelve. Planning for the birth is pure beautiful, man. Ah mean, getting up the duff is a nightmare cos you cannae get the hair extensions or drink, man, or take drugs or get your highlights done – well, that's what they tell you.

All it really means is a trip tae the pram centre near the Barras for a fake Burberry pushchair and carry oan as normal. Ah wouldn't change it for anything. Ah've got brilliant weans and grandweans and we're a complete family now. Ah pure feel sorry for my pal, Paris Milton. She's thirty-nine and she's still no' a granny! Pure fuckin' mental, man.

See that posh guy, the publisher, man, he says we've got a better chance of selling oor book if we make people laugh. So here's a collection of jokes we got from oor mates and stuff. Keanu wants more accessories on the Corsa and Ah want pure big tits so the more royalties we get, the better, man.

Paris Milton gave us loads of jokes about dating and bus stops and that. She thinks she's pure funny, man, but she's actually a pure whore but we're still best mates, know what Ah mean, man? She reckons she's going tae adopt one of those Romanian babies. She's pure raging that she's no' a granny yet. It's amazing really cos her daughter is pure dick-daft.

Ah don't get all the jokes in the book, man, but Keanu says that's because Ah'm blonde but he's the stupid one cos ma hair's really black . . .

A thirteen-year-old nedette goes to the doctor and says she thinks she might be pregnant. The doctor examines her and says, 'Congratulations! I can confirm you most certainly are pregnant!' And the nedette says, 'Oh, fuck. Is it mine?'

Billy from Bridgeton shags a thirteen-year-old nedette in Torremolinos. Upon her return home, she goes to the doctor who confirms that she is indeed up the duff. Her main worry is that the child might have a Spanish accent.

Where would a ned go on a first date?
A bus shelter.

What do you call a nedette with a
reputation for being easy?
Full.

Shuggy and Graham were in the local pub having a game of pool after a hard day signing on at the buroo.

Shuggy went for a slash when he noticed that the condom machines had been refilled with new flavoured johnnies. The thought of surprising his wife, Kelly-Marie, when he got home was too great so he bought a pack of three assorted flavours.

Back home, a few hours later, Kelly-Marie is well chuffed with her husband's new purchase and suggests they go upstairs, get naked and turn out the lights so she can guess the different flavours.

Minutes later they're in the bedroom naked, lights out, when she says, 'Three cheeses.'

Shuggy says, 'Gie's a minute to get it oan first.'

What do you call two neds having a sixty-nine?
Odour eaters.

What does a nedette say after multiple orgasms?
That was pure brilliant, team.

What do neds use for birth control with non-neds?
Their personalities.

A rather nervous ned goes round to his burd's house to collect her before going to the local park for a night of snogging and Buckie drinking. As Nicole isn't ready he sits in the living room with her parents, all three of them enjoying a can of Super, although there are awkward silences. Just as he finishes his drink, the family Rottweiler wakes up and starts licking his balls.

'Aw, cool, man, Ah wish Ah could dae that,' shouts the ned.

'Well, gie him a biscuit and Ah'm sure he'll let ye,' says the ma as she drains her can.

What does a ned do when his burd starts smoking?
He slows down and uses lubrication.

What would a ned do if he wanted to lose weight
to impress his burd on their second date?
He'd walk on to the next bus shelter.

Did you hear about the nedette who asked the surgeon if her ned boyfriend would be any good at foreplay after his operation?

'Of course he will,' the surgeon replied.

'That's good,' the nedette mused. 'He was nae good at it before.'

What do a clitoris, an anniversary and
a lavvy have in common?
A ned will always miss them.

Why don't nedettes blink during sex?
It's over so fast, they don't have time.

What's the difference between 'ooh' and 'haw'?
About two inches.

What's the difference between a can
of Special Brew and a G-spot?
Neds will spend hours searching for
a can of Special Brew.

Why do nedettes wear pants?
To keep their ankles warm.

Why do nedettes wear G-strings?
To keep their ankle chains warm.

What's the definition of ned trust?
A blow job.

What's a nedette's favourite nursery rhyme?
Hump me, dump me.

What's the difference between a nedette and
the Grand Old Duke of York?
The Grand Old Duke of York only
had ten thousand men.

What do a nedette and a Buckie bottle
have in common?
They're both empty from the neck up.

How does a nedette turn out the lights before sex?
She closes the car door.

What do you call a thirty-year-old nedette?
Dunno, ask her seventeen-year-old son.

What do a ned and a drum have in common?
The more you bang it, the looser it gets.

What do you call neds in a bus shelter?
A party.

What have nedettes got in common with turtles?
When they're on their back, they're fucked.

What do you call a twelve-year-old ned?
Daddy.

What do you call a twenty-four-year old ned?
Grandad.

Newly-wed neds, Jason and Amy, arrive at the hotel reception desk to book a room telling the receptionist that they just got married that afternoon. The receptionist congratulates them, quotes the room rates and asks if they'd like the bridal. Jason politely refuses saying, 'Nae need, ta, Ah can hold her by the ears until she gets the hang of it.'

A newly-wed ned couple arrive at their honeymoon Travelodge when the young nedette bride, still in her white shellsuit, tells her new husband Boab that she's still a virgin.

Outraged, Boab storms out and goes home to his family. In the morning, when he can finally explain to his family what the problem was, his mother says, 'A virgin! That's ridiculous that, if she's no' good enough for her ain family she's no' good enough for you.'

What does a nedette mother say to her
daughter before she goes on a date?
'If you're not in bed by twelve, come home.'

A pregnant nedette, Nicole, is sat in front of the telly,
watching *Corrie*, when she looks over at Hamilton.

'Haw, man!' she says.

Hamilton sighs and puts down his Buckie, 'Whit is it,
Nicole?'

'I could just go some snails!' she says.

'Snails!' Hamilton cries. 'For fucksake. This is Pilton,
no' the Champs Elysées! You and your cravings. Where
am Ah gonnae get snails? And at this time of night! Whit
the fuck dae you want snails for, anyway? You and me
have never had snails!'

'You'd get them for me if you loved me,' Nicole says,
giving him the cow eyes and blinking furiously.

'Aye, OK,' Hamilton says.

'It's only hauf seven, anyway,' Nicole says.

Hamilton stands up and makes for the door. He
doesn't know where on earth to look for snails, so he
decides the best thing to do is to ask his mates in the
Shieldaig Inn.

'Haw! Big yin!' his mates cry as Hamilton wanders in.
'We've no' seen you for weeks, man! A pint of Stella for
the big yin!'

Hamilton is overjoyed to be allowed out and enjoys his
first pint of Stella in months, followed by three pints of

cider. After another three pints, the boys all listen to Hamilton's challenge. Davey rubs his chin and Malkie's at a loss to know where to find snails in Pilton on a wet Wednesday night, or any night, wet or dry or pure pishin' doon, come to that.

'Whit about Tesco's, man?' Rabbie suggests.

'The chip shop?' Brian pipes up.

'Haw, man! How about the Spar on the corner, man? You can always get some fags and Buckie instead if there's no snails. Or prawns, man. They're similar are they no'? She'll never know the difference, will she?'

Joe decides he's heard some requests from pregnant girlfriends in the past, but never one as tough as this, and gets his round in while they give it some more thought. This dilemma causes the boys some consternation and they discuss the problem, among others, while they each sink another five pints. It gets to closing time and the boys are stoating up the road, cheerfully putting the world to rights. They all go off to their houses leaving Hamilton on his own to go up his drive.

As he tries to unlock the gate and weave up the path, Hamilton sees the light go on and immediately goes into action. The front door is suddenly flung wide open.

'Hamilton!' Nicole shouts. 'Whit time dae you call this and where on earth have you been?'

She peers into the front garden to see Hamilton bent double, whooshing his arms towards the front door, staring intently at the ground shouting, 'Snails! Snails! Snails!'

What do neds use for protection during sex?
A bus shelter.

A nine-year-old ned asked his mother, 'Why am Ah ginger and you're no'?'

'Don't even ask,' she replied. 'When Ah think back to that fuckin' party, you're lucky you don't bark.'

Three neds walked into a bar, sat down with three pints of lager and started bragging about how they had given their new girlfriends duties. The first man had moved in with a Catholic nedette from the east end of Glasgow. He bragged that he had told his woman she was to do all the dishes and house cleaning that needed doing at his place. He said it took a couple days but on the third day he came home to a clean house and the dishes were all wished and put away.

The second man had set up house with a Protestant nedette from Partick. He bragged that he had given his girlfriend orders that she was to do all the cleaning, the dishes and the cooking. He told them the first day he didn't see any results but the next day it was better. By the third day, his house was clean, the dishes were done and he had a huge dinner on the table.

The third man had moved in with a Jewish nedette from the south side of Glasgow. He boasted that he told her that her duties were to keep the house clean, dishes wished, lawn mowed, laundry done and hot meals on the table, every day. He said the first day he didn't see anything, the second day he didn't see anything but by the third day most of the swelling had gone down and he could see a little out of his left eye.

Dylan, a little ned, asks for a bike for his birthday. His dad says, 'We'd get you one but oor mortgage is fifty thousand pounds and your mum has lost her job.'

Next day, little Dylan walks out with his suitcase packed. His dad asks, 'Where are you going, son?'

Little Dylan replies, 'Ah walked past your bedroom last night and heard you tell mum you were pulling oot. Then Ah heard mum tell you to wait cos she was coming too. Ah'm not staying here on me own with a fifty-thousand mortgage and no fuckin' bike!'

Wee Andy and his mates were all at the SECC carnival and got chatting to a group of nedettes. Before long wee Andy and Michaela were snogging by the waltzers and Michaela suggested going back to her place as her ma and da were on holiday in Portobello and her social worker wasn't due until the following morning.

Soon things were getting heavy and they were stripping each other's trackies off as they made their way to the bedroom. Wee Andy was amazed at the amount of furry toys she had. They were everywhere, on the bed, furniture and the window ledge – in fact it was like something from a fairground.

The passion increased and they shagged each other senseless. Then they finished the session off by sparking up a Mayfair and smoking it between them. Wee Andy asked how he had performed and Michaela said, 'You can choose something from the bottom shelf.'

A ned shagging his burd says, 'Bend over. We'll try the social security position.'

'Whit the fuck is that?' she says.

'When ma balls touch your arse, you're getting full benefit.'

What does a nedette's right leg say to her left leg?
Nothing, they've never met.

What do you call a nedette who's lost
ninety per cent of her intelligence?
Single.

A peroxide nedette and her spiral-permed pal are talking one day. The spiral-permed pal says her boyfriend has a dandruff problem but she gave him 'Head and Shoulders' and it cleared up. So the peroxide nedette says, 'How do you give shoulders?'

Why do neds have orgasms?
So they know when to stop shagging.

How do you know if a ned is sexually active?
He's got a pulse.

How do you get a nedette pregnant?
Come on her shoes and let the flies do the rest.

Three nedettes meet in the doctor's waiting room. To make conversation, the first nedette says, 'Ah'm going to have a boy cos Ah was on top.'

The second nedette says, 'Ah'm having a girl because Ah was on the bottom.'

The third nedette bursts into tears and says, 'Ah'm having puppies.'

Kevin went to the doctor concerned about his discoloured penis. The doctor examined him and asked, 'Is there perhaps a family history of yellow genitals?'

Kevin assured the doctor there wasn't.

The doctor asked Kevin if he worked with dangerous chemicals and again Kevin said no as he was typically unemployed.

'So what do you do all day?' asked the doctor.

'Ah usually watch pornos and eat Quavers.'

A nedette is in labour and dials 999 for an ambulance. The operator says, 'Are you sure this is an emergency? Do you really need an ambulance?'

'Aye, ma fuckin' waters huv broke.'

'Sorry, I didn't realise,' replies the operator. 'Where are you ringing from?'

'Where do you think? Fae ma fanny tae ma feet,' replies the nedette.

A ned went to see his burd in hospital. She'd given birth to triplets. The ned looked them over, turned to the nurse and said, 'We'll keep the wan in the middle, man.'

What's the mating call of a nedette?
'Ah'm pure pished, man.'

Haw, man, Jason, gonnae tell him tae shut the door? I pure cannae dae it wi' folk watching.

Lee proposes to Donatella and she accepts. He's really happy and hands her a small diamond. 'Whit the fuck's that?' screams Donatella.

'It's an unmounted stone – it'll be mounted the day after you are, doll.'

Dale and Wayne are on the way to an Old Firm match, having a chat, when Dale says that he wishes his burd had never got a part-time job. Now she's let the whole family down by working for a living and she's always too tired for nookie – he's lucky if he gets any twice a week. 'Twice a week, man?' says Wayne. 'No' bad, she's cut some of us back tae just the once.'

A newly married ned couple are arguing about how many kids to have.

'Ah want four,' says Sammie-Jo.

'Ye're on tae plums, hen, three's mare than enough. Four weans'll cost a fuckin' fortune.'

'Aye well, Ah hope you'll love the fourth as if it were one of yer ain then, ya stingy big streak of piss.'

How do you make a nedette scream after an orgasm?
Wipe your dick on her plasma-screen telly.
She doesn't care about the sheets – they
haven't been changed for weeks.

Two neds are in the back row of the cinema snogging passionately. Eventually Ryan says, 'Look Sheryl, will ye stop passing me yer chewing gum!'

'Aw, that's no' chewing gum. Ah've got bronchitis.'

Two neds are sharing a bottle of Buckie down on Clydeside. Eventually the conversation turns to their sexual conquests.

'So do you use a condom when ye shag yer burd?' asks the first ned.

'Durex?'

'Naw, come oan, man, Ah asked you first.'

What does a nedette put behind her ears
to make her more attractive?
Her ankles.

A man standing at the back of a crowded hotel lift shouts, 'Ballroom, please.'

The nedette standing in front turns to him and says, 'Aye, aw right, there's nae need tae boast.'

How do you castrate a ned?
Kick his burd on the back of the head.

A ned and nedette go back to her parents' house after a night down the pub. It's their first date and they're really nervous. But she assures the ned that her ma and da will be well asleep by the time they go back. 'Just don't make a noise, right, as they'll come doon.'

Things get rocking on the sofa but the ned suddenly realises the booze has got the better of him and he needs to use the bathroom.

'Aw, man,' the nedette moans. 'You cannae go upstairs. Just use the kitchen sink, right.'

So the ned goes through to the kitchen. A few minutes later he reappears around the door, trousers round his ankles.

'Haw, Kelly!'

'Whit?'

'You got any toilet paper or will Ah just use the J-cloth?'

A dyed-blonde nedette walks into a bar, stotious.

'Haw, man! Have you seen Grigor?'

The barman looks at her and says, 'Aye, he was here an hour ago.'

The nedette stares at him, trying to focus.

'Was Ah wi' him?' she asks.

Why are nedettes like carpets?
Because, if a ned lays her the right way first time, he'll walk all over her for the rest of her life.

What's the difference between a ned's
life and a ned's wife?
After twenty-five years, the ned's life still sucks.

Why does a nedette have two holes?
So when she gets plastered, you can
carry her like a six pack.

Why is a nedette like a chicken farmer?
Because both of them raise cocks
pretty much full time.

What two things in the air can
make a nedette pregnant?
Her legs.

What do you call that useless piece of
skin around a nedette's pussy?
A nedette.

Why are nedettes like screen doors?
Once they get banged a few times, they
loosen up.

Why is a nedette like a door knob?
Every one gets a turn.

How can you tell when a nedette is dating?
There's a buckle print on her forehead.

What words does a ned not want to
hear when he's having sex?
'Excuse me, when's the next bus to
Princes Street due?'

Why does a nedette get married in a white trackie?
So she can fit in with all the other
kitchen appliances.

What's worse than a ned chauvinist pig?
A nedette who won't do what she's told.

Why did God give neds penises?
So they'd have at least one way
to shut nedettes up.

What's the difference between a ned's unemployment
benefit and his dick?
He doesn't have to ask a nedette to blow his
unemployment benefit.

What's six-inches long, three inches
wide and drives a nedette wild?
A five pound note.

What's the most active muscle
in a nedette's body?
A penis.

Why do most neds die before their women?
Because they want to.

What's the best thing about a nedette
giving a blow job?
thirty seconds of silence.

A nedette who has just given birth jumped out of bed to
use the loo. On the way back, in her robe, she walks into
the main entrance, up to the information desk and asks
to use the phone directory for Edinburgh – Bruntsfield

or Marchmont – the poshest bits she'd heard of. So the manager looks at her wrecked state, thin cheeks and chicken-hip body and asks her why she is out of bed.

'Ah want to search through the phone book and find a name for ma wean,' the nedette explains.

'I see,' says the manager. 'Well, look, why don't you go back to bed and ask your family for a name book? They have lovely books these days. In fact, I think there is one in the maternity ward. You could ask to have a look at that with the baby's father.'

'Haw, man! You dinnae understand,' replies the nedette. 'Ah'm looking for a second name. Ma baby already has a first name.'

Why are neds and spray paint alike?
One squeeze and they're all over you.

Two nedette grandmas are talking in Somerfield. 'Whit do you think it means when a woman comes back to a man who's sober, kind, considerate and affectionate?'

'Dunno.'

'It means she's in the wrang hoose.'

A ned receives a call to say that his mother-in-law has died, aged thirty-three. They want to know if the mother-in-law would have wished to be buried or cremated.

The ned replies, 'Dinnae take any chances. Burn the body and bury the ashes, man!'

What to say to a nedette in the pub . . . I'd really love to screw your brains out but it looks like someone beat me to it.

How do you make your nedette scream
out loud when you're having sex?
Phone her and let her know what she's missing.

Have you heard about the new,
sensitive condoms for nedettes?
They hang around and talk to her once
the ned has left the bus shelter.

How do you know when a nedette
achieves orgasm?
She drops her chips.

How do you know when a nedette is
sexually excited and getting it on?
She puts down her nineteen-inch pizza and
oven chips for a minute.

How do you know when a ned achieves orgasm?
The nedette's just started her chips.

A ned and nedette are out on their first date in the bus shelter. Things are hotting up and, as he starts to remove her white hoodie, she says, 'Slow doon, man, not so fast . . . Ah've never done this before. Now that we've been going oot for an hour and we're getting serious, can you tell me whit a penis is?'

So the ned says, 'Aye, nae bother, hen!' as he lobs it out.

So she says, inspecting it, 'Oh, right, it's like a dick but smaller.'

Two nedettes are walking along the road past a burnt-out van on their way to school, chatting away about the previous night when they had a foursome with twin brothers and one of them starts to cry.

'Whit's up wi' you?' asks Chantelle.

'Ah always get sentimental when Ah see the place that Ah lost my virginity.'

Jade, a nedette, gets married to Damien, a ned, and they have the party at her house. Her ma, who is pure horny as a result of Jade's da being deid these past six years, puts the finishing touches to the banquet she's laid on in the living room. Jade is sixteen, an only child and still very innocent. She's just come out of the convent school where her ma sent Jade to protect her. Her ma boasts about Jade all the time, on account of her being brought up to respect family values, and about Damien, who she says is the catch of a lifetime at sixteen, because he's just started taking driving lessons. So Jade's ma goes into the kitchen and starts heating up the pizza bites and the oven-ready chips.

Jade comes down to the kitchen after only half an hour and cries to her ma, 'Ma! He's taking his claes off!' Jade's ma, excited at the thought but not letting on, shouts, 'Get back up there, Jade. That's normally what men do on their wedding night.'

So Jade goes back upstairs, only to reappear after five minutes. 'Haw, Ma! His chest is pure hairy, by the way, and Ah'm pure worried at what Ah'm seeing!'

Jade's ma is on heat by now but she tries to stay calm. 'Och, take your time, Jade! Ah've still to take those pavlovas oot of the freezer, by the way.'

So Jade climbs the stairs yet again but is back in the doorway after four minutes. Jade is pure white faced after suffering a terrible fright, having just found out that Damien had a traumatic car accident as a child, when stealing a motor, and had to be cut out of the Mercedes leaving just a stump on his right leg.

Jade's Ma turns to Jade and says, 'Whit is it Jade?' She's pure got her own eye on Damien's da in the next room.

'Ma! Damien's taken his trousers off and he's got a foot and a half!'

Jade's ma drops her tea towel and the pavlova box as she plumps up her hair and renews her lipstick. 'A foot and a half? Jade! Oot the way!' she cries, as she stampedes up the stairs.

One ned asks his friend, 'Why does your wife speak through her nose like that?'

He replies, 'Cos she's worn her mouth out!'

What's the difference between a
nedette and a wheelie bin?
You only need to take the wheelie
bin out once a week.

Did you hear about the lonely ned who went to buy a packet of condoms?

He was last seen outside Haddows alone with his Mates.

A Quick Guide For Girls

You know you've met a ned when . . .

The day was a total waste of make-up.

It sounds like English but you can't understand a word he's saying.

He's so thick he can't count to twenty-one unless he's got his trackie bottoms off.

He only travels in a pack.

He had a thought once but it died of loneliness.

He spits at you.

He starts running at the sound of a police siren.

He'll never make *Who's Who?* but he qualifies for *What's That?*

He had feelings once – aged three.

You ask him the time and he's told you everything he knows.

He couldn't even win Best of Breed at Cruft's.

His IQ is rivalled only by that of your garden gnome. (No, you don't have one.)

He's got the personality of a wet firework on Guy Fawkes Night.

You don't know what his problem is but it's hard to pronounce.

He thinks the world's out to get him – it is, get over it.

He likes vinegar – for his cuts and bruises.

You walk into the only Kentucky Fried Chicken in the Sahara and there he is.

The fillings in his teeth have been replaced with chewed-up crisps.

His favourite food is bar snacks. (eighty-seven per cent of all bar snacks have traces of urine on them.)

He's not drunk – he just likes to leave a stranger's car in a different stranger's garden.

He's not drunk – he just lives in a bus shelter.

He's not pissed – he always parks around a tree.

His most stable relationships are with burgers, bus shelters and the local polis.

You thought it was a date until he invited you back to his bus shelter.

He regularly holds on to the pavement to stop himself from sliding off the Earth.

He's only fourteen.

He says, 'He kept looking at me so Ah bit him.'

He says, 'He kept looking at me so Ah smashed a Buckie bottle over his heid.'

He says, 'Ah hit her cos she was a Goth.'

He's sitting at the back of a bus, upstairs, with a pack of ned mates and he's surrounded by spit.

If his IQ was higher, he'd be a Rottweiler.

He's having a party in his head but no one else is invited.

If brains were taxed, the government would get a refund.

His head whistles in a cross wind.

A Quick Guide For The Boys

You know she's a nedette if . . .

Her tattoos are more all over her than her clothes.

She's lost at least one tooth opening a beer bottle.

She lives on Pro Plus, Red Bull and black coffee.

Her toilet paper has numbered sheets.

She hammers his beer bottle tops into the doorframes to make them look pretty.

Her car is parked in the front garden and has no wheels.

She humps you and dumps you.

She does her spring cleaning by calling in the council who arrive wearing masks.

Her wedding ring is a sovereign one and she got married in a white tracksuit.

She wears her kid's picture in a hologram around her neck.

She asks you how fast you can open a locked car – which beats her record for turning her house key in its lock.

2

Ned Cars
by Keanu

To earn the respect of other ned drivers you have to disobey most of the laws and have no respect for any other road-users. Cyclists are a pure classic target, man, for scaring the shit out of. That Clydeside Expressway, Clydebank and the roundabout at Milngavie are the places to hang out and intimidate them, brilliant, man.

And we take oor music seriously, by the way. Kylie is taking the piss cos Ah spent five grand on modifications to the Punto, including a stereo system that takes up the whole boot. It's dead important that people can hear your tunes and exhaust before they see you. That way they can pure anticipate the motor coming towards them. Only thing is now Ah've got an ASBO cos the neighbours kept complaining about the noise so Ah can't park the motor near the house after 10 p.m.

The best place to see neds in cars, man, is at the Strathycruise on a Sunday night. Me and Kylie go quite often and cruise in the Punto but the traffic can be pure murder, man. There's hundreds of cars on show, all totally souped-up but it's what we love to spend oor cash on, even if it means spending all oor benefits at once. The louder the exhaust, the more the burds pure fancy you.

Blacked-out windaes are a must-have accessory for any boy racer in the naughties. The more souped-up the motor, the more naughtie-ness there is, if you know what Ah mean?

Crash got himself a Saxo and spent six grand doing it up. He's got blue neon lighting under the motor, man, and hubcaps that spin when the car is stopped at traffic lights that he got sent over from New York. He's taken it too far, man, it's pure tasteless and tacky, if you ask me.

I just got myself a new motor, man. My mate Beaver got jailed for five years and his ma wanted it out her way. Pure bargain, by the way. Two-year-old Corsa in metallic blue. It was originally flash red but it's a ringer, man. Ah'm pure gonnae pimp up ma ride but it costs money so all the cash Ah make from this book will go on the motor.

Crash and Beaver are quality mates and we're always pissin' ourselves laughing. The two of them pure helped with the chuckles in this chapter, even though Beaver's in the Bar-L. Mind you, it's not the first time Ah've walked out the jail totally laughing, man. Ah just hope Beaver's ma doesn't buy him a copy for his Xmas, we don't want to be parting with any dosh in his direction, know what Ah mean, man?

The Ferrari formula team sacked their pit crew. The announcement came as Ferrari decided to employ Glaswegians in the pit. The decision to hire them was made after the bosses saw a documentary highlighting unemployed youths in the local area. The youths in question were able to remove a set of wheels in under five seconds without proper equipment, whereas Ferrari's existing crew took over seven seconds using hi-tech equipment. As speed in the pit from the technical teams loses or wins a race, the unemployed Glaswegians could do a sterling job. Ferrari however got more than it bargained for because, at their first practice session, the Glasgow neds successfully removed the wheels in under five seconds, re-sprayed, re-badged and sold the vehicle to McLaren for four bottles of Buckie, two cans of Tennents and a kilo of hash.

A nedette is driving home from a hen night a little the worse for wear when she's spotted by the police driving erratically. The policeman signals her to pull over and asks her to take a breathalyser test, which she does.

He looks at the result and says, 'You've obviously had a good night. Looks like you've had more than one stiff one.'

'Oh, officer, can you tell that from the test too?'

What do you call a ned in a car?
Arrested.

What do you call a ned in a Porsche?
A thief.

NED CARS

What's a ned's favourite car?
One without an alarm.

Why does a ned constantly rev his engine?
So it doesn't cut out.

What do you call a ned killed by a boy racer?
A good start to the day.

What do you do if you run over a ned?
Put the car into reverse – just to make sure.

You're in your car and you see a ned on a
bike. Why should you avoid him?
It might be your bike.

Two neds in a car without any
music, who's driving?
The police.

Why is three neds in a head-on
collision in a Punto a waste?
A Punto could seat five.

How do you get one hundred neds
into a phone box?
Paint three stripes on the side.

How do unemployed neds travel?
By ambulance and taxi . . .

A ned was driving his dad's old Capri through Leith when he hit a hare. A passing nedette, on the pavement, shrieked and rushed over as the ned stopped.

'Look at ma car,' the ned said.

'Never mind that,' said the nedette. 'That hare belongs to the chief of polis in Leith.'

'Fucksake,' said the ned. 'WhatamAhgonnae dae?' He was close to tears. 'Ah'll get banged up – Ah haven't asked if Ah can borrow this car.'

'Tell you what,' the nedette said, opening her pink bag from Morgan. 'Use this.'

She handed him a can and he looked at it.

'Spray the hare,' she said.

'Hare's fuckin' dead, man,' the ned informed her.

'Just spray it, right?'

The ned looked at her and at the can, then at the hare, lying there, limp.

'Ah'm no going down for graffitting the chief of polis's pet – that dead hare,' the ned protested.

'Naw, man, just spray him, right?'

The ned cracked open three cans of Red Bull, drank them, then sprayed the hare with the contents of the can the nedette handed him. She stood and watched. Suddenly the hare jumped on to all fours, held up a paw in salute to the ned and sprinted off round the block. The ned stood staring, amazed at the change in the hare.

Suddenly the hare reappeared, on its second run round the block, held up a paw again and waved at the ned and nedette. The ned looked open-mouthed at the nedette and watched as the hare circled once more and threw up both paws in a Mexican wave and disappeared.

'Whit the fuck was in that can, man?' the ned asked the nedette.

So the nedette said, 'Read the tin.'

The ned looked down at the can in his hand and read the words out loud, 'Hairspray – adds life to dead hair. With permanent wave.'

A ned walks into a bar in Fountainbridge and orders three Strongbows. He realises after a long night, when he goes outside, that his car has been hot-wired and nicked. Bold and fired up by the Strongbow, he goes back into the pub. He shouts as he walks in, 'Haw! Which one of you c**ts stole ma car?'

No one spoke.

'OK then, Ah'm gonna have another Strongbow and if ma car's not outside by the time Ah finish, Ah'm gonna dae what Ah did in Leith, man. And Ah don't like tae dae what Ah did in Leith.'

Some of the locals shift uncomfortably in their seats. The ned, true to his word, finishes his Strongbow and walks outside. His car has been returned. The ned gets into the car and starts the engine. The barman saunters out of the pub and up to the ned.

'Ho! Big man!' he calls. 'What happened in Leith?'

The ned turns to him and says through the open window, 'Ah had tae walk home.'

A traffic cop sees a car being driven erratically along the Meight at Harthill. He pulls over the driver, a teenage lad in head-to-toe Burberry, and asks him to blow into the breathalyser.

'Sorry mate, no can do. Ah'm asthmatic, man, by the way.'

When asked for a urine sample he also refuses saying he'd just gone for a slash five minutes before. A further request for a blood sample back at the polis station is also refused as he is a haemophiliac and could bleed to death. Losing patience, the officer demands that he walk the white line.

'Whit are you oan? Ah'm no doin' that, man, no fuckin' way. Ah'm too pished,' replies the ned.

Delaney is driving through the Clyde Valley, showing off his new motor to his girlfriend Chrystal, when he slows down to let another car cross a narrow bridge. The other driver shouts 'cow' as he passes and outraged at his burd being insulted, Delaney shouts back, 'Get it up ye, ya wee fucker!' Delaney, foot to the floor, crosses the bridge and hits a cow in the middle of the road head-on.

Kimberley is taking her driving test and things are going well. The examiner says, 'When I hit the dashboard with my folder I want you to stop as if a small child has run out in front of you, do you understand?'

'Aye,' she replies and the examiner duly hits the dashboard.

The car screeches to a halt as Kimberley does a hand-brake stop and gets out of the car screaming, 'Huv ye nae road sense, ya silly wee bastard? Wait tae Ah see yer ma!'

Wee Kevin is walking home from his gran's when a car slows down and the driver offers him a bag of sweeties to get in. Kevin refuses and keeps walking. The driver offers him two bags of sweeties. Again Kevin refuses. The driver offers him two bags of sweeties and a tenner. Again Kevin refuses. The driver is exasperated and offers Kevin all the sweeties he wants, a tenner and a Playstation game. 'No way, Da,' says Kevin, 'Ah told ye, Ah'm no' gettin' intae a stolen motor wi' you ever again.'

A boy racer is out cruising with his mates and a night of showing off to the ladies. He's driving slowly but goes straight through a stop sign. A traffic cop spots him and pulls him over but the boy racer is adamant that he's done nothing wrong.

'Stopped or slowed down, whit does it matter, man, Ah never hit anything so calm yer jets, officer.'

At that the policeman pulls out his truncheon and starts to beat the lad. 'So, Sonny Jim, does stopped or slowed down mean the same thing now?'

A businesswoman and a boy racer are involved in a road accident. It's particularly nasty, both cars are written off but amazingly neither of them are injured, in fact not even scratched.

After they've crawled from the wreckage of their vehicles, the woman says, 'You're a very good-looking young man and I'm a single woman, how interesting. And just look at our cars, my BMW is wrecked and your Saxo is unrecognisable but, fortunately for both of us, we're unhurt. This must be a sign that we're meant to be lovers and see each other off and on for sexual gratification.'

'Haw, totally, doll,' replied the ned, looking the woman up and down. He can't believe his luck.

The woman driver, a little shaken, reaches into her car and retrieves a bottle of wine that survived the crash and hands it to her new admirer to steady his nerves. The ned opens the bottle, necks more than half of it and hands it back to her. The woman takes the bottle, puts the cork back in and hands it back to the ned who asks why she's not having any.

The woman replies, 'No, I think I'll wait until the police have been, thanks.'

Calvin, a young ned, is walking the West Highland Way as part of his community service. He hasn't eaten properly in a few days and is desperate for a microwaved meal so he knocks on the door of a farmhouse. The farmer answers and Calvin says, 'Scuse me, man, but Ah huvnae had anythin' decent tae eat in days, can ye make me some food?'

The farmer isn't keen to give him something for nothing. He asks the ned if can go round the back and give his Clio, in the barn, a good going over. So the ned re-appears after five minutes looking flushed but rather cocky. The farmer is surprised that he's finished so quickly and asks how he found the car. The ned said that she wasn't in the barn, she was milking the cow outside and that she seemed a bit surprised to be taken from behind but it was over so quickly she didn't even drop her bucket and the udders weren't the only thing that were chugged.

What's the last thing to go through a
ned's head when he crashes through
the windscreen of his Punto?
His arse.

A ned comes out of the pub and walks to his go-faster Punto. A policeman is watching him and approaches as the ned attempts to slam the door and drive off.

'Excuse me, sonny. You're not really going to drive this car, are you?'

'Haw, see me, man?' replied the ned, vomiting on the policeman's shoes. 'Aye, Ah am, no bother. Ah'm in no condition to hot-wire a Porsche tonight, man.'

A ned was driving his burd along the road and they went over a traffic-calmed area at the back of Sighthill. 'See those road rumble strips?' said the nedette.

'Aye,' replied the ned.

'Dae you know what they're for?'

'Aye,' the ned said. 'But dae you?'

'Aye,' the nedette nodded. 'They're for when blind drivers drive over them so they know a corner's coming up.'

A ned in his Nova, on a day out to Callander, challenges a farmer in Fife who is holding up the traffic while his cows leave one field and go to another.

'How big's your farm, man?' the ned calls to him, teasing him in a nasal drone.

'Two thousand acres,' the farmer calls back, in a friendly manner.

'Haw! That's nothing, man. Ah can drive my car all day and not reach the fence on ma old man's land,' the ned taunts him.

'I feel for you,' said the farmer. 'My Mercedes is fine but I had a car like yours once.'

Two dyed-blonde nedettes are in the Punto, driving down Princes Street. Tracey goes through a red light, and then another. Sharon peers up at the traffic lights to check it was red and then stares at Tracey, who is concentrating hard on the road. She's not on the phone, not texting or drinking a bottle of Buckie. She's got both hands on the wheel and feet on the pedals.

After Tracey goes through the third red light and almost collides with a Number 1 bus, Sharon coughs and says, 'Tracey, man, was that a red light back there?'

'Fuck, man!' Tracey shouts. 'Am Ah driving?'

3

Ma Life as a Ned . . .
by Skid (brother of Crash and Bern Markes)

See me this mornin'? Ah was driving the Punto, man, and there was this tube on a bike, man. He was a real twat in yellow, man, going, like, really slow round the roundabout and that. Pure mental. So Ah drove at him, man, to get him oot ma road. He was so frighted he fell aff, man, and Ah drove aff pishin' masel'. Gied the bloke the wanker sign at one hundred miles an hour, man. He looked like a dead wasp lying there. Pure mince, man. Reminded me of the time we went to Saltcoats.

I picked up this burd down the fair. We broke into a beach hut cos it was pure pishin' doon, man. Went hard at it all night, man, and it was only next mornin' Ah realised we'd been lying on dead wasps all night. Hunners of them. Ah thought the crunchy floor was just sand. It was pure revolting, man. She was lying in it though, man. Glad it wasnae me. Plus the burd was sick, over my white trackies, threw up purple stuff everywhere, man, turned ma gut so much Ah spewed ma ring too. That was pure vomit. Disgusting, man, puttin' they trackies back on and having to walk back and find ma ma and da. Ma head was stonkin', man. Ah was gonna ditch her, man, but she was beggin' me not tae. She was still sick, so Ah found the auld yins.

We went tae this caff, man. My da was still steamin' from the night before and he wanted something sweet. He's got no teeth, had most of them knocked out in a fight wi' big Eddie over a bet he lost. So he went aff to find the toilet and we gied him this huge banana split, man, put it on the table for when he came back. He starts eating it and Ah thought Ah'd get the boak, man, as he goes, 'Mmmn, mmmn, mmmn, this is really nice.' Only it was made out of lard and wax, man. We'd got it aff the display as you went in. He didnae guess – he was fleein', man.

This burd, the waitress, comes over and she's ending herself, man. Says, 'Can Ah get you another?' Ah could have had her, man – thought about getting her into the lads' bogs but we had to get the old man intae the car. That burd who was throwin' up, man, and lying in the wasps – she was still there. Then ma old man gets in the car, man, and he throws up everywhere. It was pure disgustin'. And it was in ma fuckin' car, man.

Ma ma was laughing so hard she said she nearly pished hersel' and then the burd I'd shagged senseless all night, man, started vomiting again. Car was pure covered in vomit. Stinking. All doon the windaes, in the air vents and have you ever tried getting the sick out of the channels of Burberry-corduroy seats, man? It was fuckin' minging. Ah had to wear the same trackies the next day. Ah tried to wash them but couldnae get them dry. They had three lots of vomit on them – hers, his and then his again. Then hers. Oh, that's four, man. Well, you know what Ah mean, man.

So Ah couldnae get them dry, man, so Ah got most of it oot and Ah heated up the iron and ironed them on masel' but Ah must have had the iron too hot cos it went through ma trackies ontae ma legs and Ah ended up in casualty with that burd. Ah had third degree burns and triangles of white nylon melted on ma legs. Ah was screamin' like a wean wi' the pain. Not as bad as ma arse-crack though, man.

When Ah was doing the ironing – on ma legs – Ah tried to watch telly and the remote wasnae workin'. Last time, when Ah was watching *Grease* (Ah've seen that film 256 times noo an' that's just this year, man), the remote was pure dodge and it was the batteries and ma old man said to heat them up. Only this was summer, so Ah put the batteries against the iron, but that didnae do it, so Ah put them in my crack, man. Only there must have been something wrong with them, leaked or something, man, cos the next thing Ah had fire up ma crack, pure burning, man, and my thighs were burning with the iron and melted trackies stuck to ma skin and Ah had to call my burd. She drove the Punto like a mad man, Ah was shittin' masel' especially when we near clipped the polis motor on Govan Road.

The Punto is still covered in the sick, man. It was stinking and that daft burd threw up again, the smell was pure vomit, man. Ah felt a bit sorry for her though, so soon as Ah was OK and oot of hospital Ah drove tae see her. Only the two-timing slag was seeing someone else. Ah went round there, man, tae her hoose, and she was seeing some other bloke by then. Ah think he was a pure poof, man – he was wearin' a pink T-shirt and ripped jeans and didn't even have a cap on! So Ah tried to get oot of there fast and reversed over her ma's front garden by mistake. Her old ma, Donna-Marie, comes pouring oot the hoose tae stop me, only Ah hit her ma's car and that ornamental wishing-well in the centre of the grass that she got fae the Shell garage for a tenner.

Ah thought her ma had took a pure heart attack, man, cos she keeled over. Turned oot she'd slipped and had an asthma attack but Ah was pure worried, by the way. Had to find her inhaler. Ah runs intae the hoose, looking for that inhaler, man, and Ah found a purple one and a twenty-pound note so Ah took that too. Reckoned she owed me that for all the sick in the car, man. Her ma's lying there in the garden, gasping, man, surrounded by skid marks on her perfect lawn, man – it was pure carved up, man, and Ah thought about shagging her. She's not a bad-looking woman for thirty-five, her ma, pure quality bit of gear, but she was on all fours on the gravel, panting and trying to get her breath and Ah thought about taking her fae behind but mebbes now was not the time. Particularly as ma car was impaled on her car, man.

It made me laugh that that boot of a burd came back with the new prick of a boyfriend and ma car was still stuck in her ma's car. Like ma car was giving her ma's car one pure doggy style, man. Ah tried to push ma car off her ma's car, cos the recovery wanted a hunner and fifty, man, and Ah only had that burd's twenty but Ah wrecked my shoulder, man, and it was totally sore. So Ah had to use their bathroom, man, and as Ah went to wipe my crack, cos the pus was seepin through my boxers, Ah felt this lightning bolt in my arm, man, and Ah couldn't move my arm from my arse. The burd's ma had to drive me back to hospital, man. Turns oot her car is still driveable and the hospital said Ah had a dislocated shoulder, man. Pure pain, man.

The ma asked me back for a drink and Ah couldnae refuse. It took a bottle of voddie to numb the pain, man. Well, she gied me a shot and went oot of the room, so Ah downed the rest, man. Straight voddie, mental. Ah wanted to look OK for her ma, as it was just me and her, man, so Ah went up to the bathroom and tried to shave, man. Only all Ah could find was her Ladyshave. Ah reckoned her man had legged it, so Ah switched it on and shaved my chin. Only it wasnae all that good, man, so Ah tried it on my legs and then – Ah don't know what happened, man, but mebbes it was the buzzing of this thing, man, or because Ah was pure steamin', but Ah stuck it in my mouth, man, and shaved my tongue. Ah had this pure buzzing in ma heid, man. Then Ah realised my tongue was all carved up, man, it was pure spraying blood all over the bathroom mirror and Ah used two bog rolls, man, nicked from her work, to pure stop the blood pishin' oot of me. A couple of ice cubes and another shot of voddie and Ah was pure sorted, man. But Ah had to get tae work, man. The car was still oot of action and Ah felt a bit pished so Donna-Marie gied me a lift in her motor.

Ah've got this job as a chef, man. Only been in it a week, though. This stoater of a burd works there, man. She's pure beautiful, by the way. Dropped her chips in the sink when Ah shagged her, man – Ah was pure embarrassed. Cos it's so hot in the kitchen and you get chef's bum, man – the ovens are scorching, man, and you cannae sit doon. They tell you to put cornflour over your crack, man, to take up all the sweat and so Ah did that, man, only they didnae have the cornflour so Ah used pure flour. By the next mornin', the flour and the hairs on ma arse had stuck together, so Ah couldnae get free without taking scissors to it and cutting them all away. Only Ah ended up in casualty again, man, cos Ah made a mess of cutting masel' and ended up with a huge gash up my crack. They had to stitch me up. That and the burns to my arse, plus my thighs, Ah was pure amazed they wee nurses at casualty didnae gie me pelters wi' the amount of times Ah've been in.

When Ah got tae work the burd Ah'd humped made me a roll wi' a burger in it – it was pure beautiful lookin' wi' sauce and onions and lettuce and that stickin' oot the sides. Ah took a bite and she was holding it, man, only when Ah bit into it Ah thought there was a bone or something in it, so Ah bit harder. It was her finger, man, and someone had to take her to casualty. It was terrible. Ah couldnae face going to casualty again, man. They know me by my first name noo, man.

Anyway, right, noo Ah'm thinkin' tae masel' that Ah'm no' cut oot for a kitchen job and I'll walk oot – get by on benefits and that, nae bother. Ah've done it before and can do it again. Ah cut across the car park when Ah meet Donna-Marie and her daughter, the burd that had spewed in the motor. Her ma was going tae the gym and sauna and said she'd take me too, a wee treat and that. It was beautiful in there. Lots of minted lookin' burds too – Ah made a mental note to get a doctor's referral and join here at a discounted rate!

Only Ah had a disaster, man. Ah was trying to be careful with all my body parts that were hurting, man, so Ah says to Donna-Marie, no funny business or fuck all. Mind you, it was nae really like that there, cos there were weans about at the pool and stuff. Anyhow, Ah'm in this sauna, man, with Donna-Marie, and Ah got very calm, man. In fact, Ah was that pure relaxed that Ah kind of revealed masel' on the bench, man. Ah was wearing very loose Lacoste shorts and one of my baws fell oot ontae one of they benches Ah was lying on. Only Ah hadnae realised and Ah got up to move too fast, cos Ah was that roasting and the thing almost tore aff. Ah was screaming with agony, man. It was pure torture. The thing was pumping the red juice and the gym called the 999, man. So this time Ah went back down to casualty in an ambulance, man, in only a pair of shorts, sweatin' like a pig and bright red, but Ah wasnae laughing. No chance of a shag that night, man.

Some of they nurses are alright though. One said to me, pure cheek like, 'You movin' in?' Ah says to her, 'No danger, doll, but I'll gie you ma moby number.' Mind you, she knew ma twin brother cos she says to me, 'Ah've had to stitch you there before.' And Ah says, 'Haw! That's my twin brother, man, Bern,' and she says, 'Aye, that's right, cos Ah was lookin' for the scar, and there was nae one.' So Donna-Marie gie's me a lift hame and before Ah crash oot, man, Ah phone my brother Bern.

My brother Bern, man, he's worse than me, man, cos he's had that part stitched, ooh, a couple of times noo. Once he went up this flagpole in a shopping centre and he caught himsel' on it, up the top. He was pure steamin', man, so when we saw the blood coming down the pole, man, we were pure feart for him. It was only when he was doon, he realised he'd ripped his tool and sack and needed four stitches (though he always says to the girls that he needed forty-four, man).

And another time he had this job, man, fixing a fence and the wummin's neighbour's dog got oot of control and tore into his behind. It was terrible. He needed twenty stitches up his jacksie. Another time, it wasnae his fault but, he was asked to fix this fence that had blew doon and he noticed the neighbours going oot. Big hooses, looked like they were all well-off punters and that, so Bern being Bern decided to see what next door had to offer. He managed to break the patio doors open wi' his tools and was just steppin' intae the sitting room and about tae home in on the plasma-screen telly when this big fuck-off Alsatian came running doon the hall towards him. He

Get a joab? Haw man, I've already goat wan – it takes skill and loads ae practice tae roll Js like these

was screamin' and pure shat himsel' but the big bastard got him and ripped his arse. (Same thing happened to him in the Bar-L once but that's another story. He'd be pure ragin' if Ah told everyone about that.)

He got away and shut the door on the dug but had to go to casualty with the arse hangin' oot his trousers and he got twenty stitches. Ah think the doctors thought it was a bit suss cos he was told to wait in a side room after they stitched him but he legged it, think they were phonin' the polis. Best bit is we don't know why he wanted the plasma screen cos we've got two at home anyway, a 42-inch wi' cinema sound and a wee portable one in the kitchen. Ma ma was ragin' cos she wants a recordable DVD to tape her soaps and shit when she's at the bingo. He could've easily have lifted that after he was bitten but naw, big poof just runs oot. He's a pure embarrassment to this family sometimes.

Reminds me of the time oor Chanelle was in Cornton Vale for shoplifting and GBH. But Chanelle's a total role model noo, goin' tae college tae study tae be a nursery nurse. No' that there's much studyin' done at nights – she's too busy oot cruisin' wi' me in the motor on nights that Ah'm no' planning on nippin' a burd. We both love goin' tae the Strathycruise at Strathclyde Park on a Sunday night.

It's a bit of a drive oot tae Motherwell but it's total quality, man. Hunners of burds for me to grope, lads for oor Chanelle and souped-up motors galore. Last week the road intae the park was jammed solid and there were a couple of hunner motors cruisin'. Magic, man. Near came in ma pants at the sights and if Ah cannae make it in person there's always a website tae chug over.

Last week I'd agreed to meet up wi' Jason, ma mate fae Wishaw wi' the silver Astra. Only he brought his newish-burd, Dannii, who it turns oot Ah'd shagged at the Barrowlands after a gig a year or so ago, but neither of us let on tae him, obviously. So we're in the car park admiring each other's motors before he decides he wants tae go on the rollercoaster. But Dannii is three months pregnant so Chanelle offers tae go with him, leaving me alone wi' Dan.

Cos Ah'm driving Ah've only got a half bottle of Buckie so we chat about the past and take a couple of swigs each from the bottle and before Ah know it we're snoggin'. Ah'm tellin' you, Ah'm pure disgusted wi' masel', getting aff with ma mate's burd but she's well up for it so what am Ah supposed tae dae? It's still daylight and Ah can see him in the queue for the rides. So Ah take Dan intae the trees and start tae take her Celtic top aff. She pulls down her white shorts and Ah just pull doon ma trackies and start tae ride her for a few minutes, got a johnnie on for safe sex and that, don't want her gettin' pregnant again.

We go back to the motor, but we get lost in the trees on the way oot and Ah hear another couple at it. Ah leave her pissin' hersel' laughin' and calling them dirty bastards to go and have a perv, when Ah see Chanelle wi' her fake Gucci bag still in her hand and her lycra mini round her waist. She's straddling Jason, giving him a ride to rival the rollercoaster, man. Even when Ah shouted, 'Ya dirty wee cow!' to her and she saw me, she never stopped, just laughed. Dan was gagging, to know what was goin' on but Ah just said it was a couple of dirty wee neds desperate for a shag. Nae need for her tae know the truth especially cos she's pregnant. Don't want her upset or anything mad like that.

Cannae believe that Jason would do the dirty on her, especially wi' her up the duff, man. Ah think Ah'm goin' tae have a word wi' him about that, pure out of order, man. If he gets oor Chanelle pregnant ma ma will pure crack up wi' him. Anyway, they two come back and are acting like the shows were the best and they had a great time so whit can Ah dae? At least Chanelle got a bit of dick oot of the trip and that's what a good night oot is all about for her. So as long as ma wee sister's happy, Ah'm happy!

Happiness doesnae last long in this family. Ma da phones the moby and it takes me a minute to find it. Ah can hear ma Eminem ringtone but Ah cannae find the fuckin' phone and Ah'm pure panicking cos it cost me 300 quid but it's in the bag wi' the Buckie bottle and johnnies. Turns oot he's been lookin after ma wee cousin Zak cos ma auntie's at the bingo wi' ma ma. Zak had tried to fill an Irn-Bru bottle wi' petrol at the local petrol station but the nozzle was too big for the bottle and he got sprayed wi' petrol. My da says he's in the Southern General.

Where the fuck does he get his brains fae? Ah know he's only nine but for fuck sake, use a funnel, wee man! So me and Chanelle have to speed off.

The Punto sounds total quality, man, when Ah boot it and Ah get ma ma and Auntie Liz-Ann tannoyed oot the bingo and take them to the Southern. Only problem is the car's pure honkin', man, cos Chanelle's pal was sick in her fake Versace clutchie the other night on the way home fae Archaos but they'll need to put up wi' it cos this is a pure emergency. It's no' the wean's fault this has happened. Ah know Liz-Ann will be straight up tae the petrol station and will have tae be held back fae assaulting the manager tonight. Ah might even phone they Health and Safety folk masel' aboot this. It's a pure liberty that a wean can be in the hospital cos someone cannae keep an eye on a petrol pump. Ah mean, dae they really think he had the money to pay for it? Eh, naw. So what if he'd filled the bottle? Would he be expected to pay for it?

We find the wean in a ward wi' others, but Liz-Ann wants him moved to a side room cos she's worried that he'll pick up an infection fae other dirty weans and we reckon that oor benefits are taxed higher than others so we're entitled to certain demands on the NHS. But that heid nurse is a pure mad-lookin' bam and there's nae way she's movin' him.

So Ah drop ma ma and Liz-Ann at the garage cos she says she's gonnae knock fuck oot the wummin at the till and we head hame tae see ma da. Well, when Ah turn intae oor street Ah cannae believe ma eyes. Oor hoose is pure rockin', man, and over the Punto's exhaust noise Ah can hear ma da on the karaoke we bought last Christmas in Argos givin' it laldy tae Robbie's 'Millennium'. Inside, the hoose is pure packed wi' mates and neighbours and it's no' like it's a celebration day, just ma da was bored and wanted company after wee Zak went oot tae play and things snowballed intae this.

No' being a family to say no to a wee party noo and then, me and Chanelle gets stuck into the cargo that's been brought and start tankin' the cider and Mad Dog before we give a wee version of 'The Locomotion' and 'Don't Look Back in Anger' – Ah pure love Oasis, man. Ah'm lovin' this party, man, total surprise and that, plus there's the bonus of Bernadette fae the next street comin' roon wi' her ma and sister cos they heard the music roon there. Bernadette's a total shag, man, a couple of ma mates have had her and she's dick-daft, so hopefully Ah'll be in there later the night, literally, man!

Ma ma and Liz-Ann appear back fae the garage just as ma da is downing his twelfth can of Super but they don't seem bothered by the party. In fact, Liz-Ann is in a good mood cos she battered fuck oot the till wummin and ma ma kept the edge for the polis so they both crack open a can themselves and take the karaoke mic and give us a blast of the Spice Girls and Sonny and Cher. Quality! This family knows how to enjoy themselves never mind what other shit's goin' on in the background, man.

Wee Zak'll be dead jealous when we tell him about the party the morra at visiting time. He looked pure lovely in his PJs and his oxygen mask. He loves a party, man. Usually he'll no' get tae his bed and it's no' the first time he's been caught draining the dregs fae other folk's glasses. He's only a wee wean but he's got tae learn aboot booze at some point so no need in makin' a big deal aboot it, especially when there's loads of fags getting left tae burn doon in ashtrays, too.

Ah remember when Ah was aboot seven year old getting tanked up and smokin' fags fae the ashtrays at a New Year party ma granny had – all the weans were doin' it. That was the last New Year party she ever had. Ah was watching from the kitchen and one of my uncles appeared pure pished just before the bells wi' his mate and his mate's da who was called Maxwell. Maxwell was still sober.

Anyways, ma granny had been a widow for a couple of weeks and was over ma granda's death, pretty much. And as Maxwell – a pure hunk of a guy – came through the door, she was pure attracted to him. She ended up snoggin' the face aff him at the bells and ma da and the rest of his brothers stopped speaking tae ma granny that night. Ah say good on her cos she was happy wi' him.

Six weeks later, Maxwell married ma granny on a beach in Benidorm. Her pal and Maxwell's ex-wife were the witnesses but the shaggin' was short-lived cos Maxwell was shot dead within hours of arrivin' hame. Seems he was the spittin' image of some gangster that was wanted by this underworld gang and that was that. Pure dead, man. Ma granny never got over it. Noo she disnae go oot much cos she thinks everyone's laughin' at her behind her back cos she married a gangster lookalike and that. We've telt her that's a load of pish but she says naw, she's made a twat of hersel' and that's that, she'll never look at another man again, but Ah'm no so sure.

She's a good-lookin' wummin for forty-six. Chanelle's tried a few times to take her to the dancin' on a Saturday night but she didn't like Archaos and wanted to go to Media but Chanelle always goes to Archaos and says she's no changin' for any auld bastard so that's put a stop to that. At least she takes pride in her appearance and that. We all go as a family tae the sunbeds – well, Ah don't go since the time Ah nearly ended up in casualty but Chanelle and ma ma and gran all go three or four times a week on they high-powered stands. Pure golden broon they are. It really sets off their blonde hair and jewellery. Ah suppose Ah've never thought aboot it much before, man, but all the lassies in ma family look the same. Yellow hair, orange tans and hunners of gold. Everyone's got a name chain – that'll be in case we forget their names when we're all pure bladdered, man.

Like the time we were all at ma big cousin Leon's funeral. He was only fifteen at the time but he got in wi' a rough crowd and they were all pished and he fell doon a manhole and drowned. Tragic, man. Ma Auntie Lana and Uncle Errol were totally gutted, man, pure greetin' and greetin' for weeks and weeks after the funeral they were.

Before the actual funeral there was a big family meetin' tae see what we thought we should be doin' to gie Leon a good send-aff. We decided he should be buried in his favourite trackie, favourite cap, new trainers wi' his socks over his trackie bottoms and we'd put in his collection of wank mags he stashed under his bed, dirty wee bastard, and his moby cos it was always stuck to his ear, his sovvy ring and the lager can he'd been drinkin' fae when he fell doon the hole (they found it next tae his body). Ma auntie and uncle were pure chuffed when they saw what we'd arranged, dead proud of Leon when they saw him lyin' there. The undertakers had done a total quality job on him, man – they even knew whit angle to put his cap oan at. Only thing they weren't keen oan was when we said we'd be bringin' a ghetto-blaster tae the church and singin' along wi' 'We Will Rock You' – Leon pure loved Queen so he'd like that wee touch tae make it mare personal and that. Ma granny cannae sing that at a karaoke any more without greetin' at the end.

We all went back tae the local Labour club after and once the booze got flowin' and the dancin' started, we all enjoyed oorsel's til the wee hoors. That was a fuckin' cracker of a funeral – we certainly know how tae see oor family aff in style, that's for sure. Lana and Errol used to watch the video of it every day but noo they've no' got time cos they've got a wee grandaughter, man. It turned oot that Leon's burd Shayla was pregnant when he died so wee Leona is a reminder to them and they pure love her and spoil her.

She's got a Burberry bag, coat and shoes, two real gold earrings in each ear, a gold bangle and blonde highlights and she's only four. Ah suppose it helps too that Shayla's moved in wi' Leon's brother Leo and noo they're a couple and Lana and Errol are pure ecstatic cos Shayla is givin' them another grandwean. As Lana said, it's no' everyone that's got two grandweans by two sons and the one mother. Ah think that makes it pure special, too. It's a heartbreakin' story, so it is, but they pure live for wee Leona so they do.

It's a hard life, man. A young lad like me thinks Ah'm getting lucky with the burds and that and, before you know it, they cause you more grief than anything else. Ah mean, you take them oot, show them a good time and meet their families and they ditch you or they can't even conduct themselves proper and that. Ah'm all for getting pure familiar with my burd's parents. Ah've got pure familiar with a few burds' mas, know what Ah mean? One time Ah was engaged to a lassie and her da was getting a bit too friendly for my liking, by the way. Ah was pure touching cloth every time Ah went round to her house and he was there.

This is a typical day in my life. Keanu thinks it's funny as fuck and you might want to read it so Ah hope you all like it and get a chuckle at ma expense.

Skid

4

Ned Funerals
by Kylie

It was pure terrible. Bern, Skid's twin and Crash's brother, pure died. He was climbing up scaffolding to get intae a wholesale jewellers in the Trongate and he slipped off when he got to the fourth floor. Tragic, man. Don't ask me why he didn't go in the front door, man – he was visiting after hours, if you know what Ah mean. Anyways, he falls aff the scaffolding and is pronounced dead at the scene so the polis go round to tell his ma but she's at the bingo. Can't imagine how it must feel to be told your wean has died and you've no' even had a win that night. She shouted, 'House!' anyway, but Ah think it was a call to her pals to go there. She waited til the end of the night, anyways. That bingo is pure dear these days. I'd be pure gutted if that was ma Britney or Darius or any of ma other weans and Ah was at the bingo.

Anyway, we helped organise the funeral for her. Keanu organised a motorcade of souped-up cars to lead the hearse and we followed in a white limo. Skid chose the songs for the church. We had 'The Lord's Prayer' and Beyoncé's 'Crazy In Love' – he'd have loved that. It was his favourite song. Ah was pure ragin' though cos the minister wouldn't let us put up the screen to show the DVD of Beyoncé, so we had to make do with just the song. Ah organised the wake in the local snooker club. We had pizza, pakora and cocktail sausages and a free bar. His ma is dead generous by the way. She paid for the cider, lager, voddie and whisky and her brother, who's a DJ, done the disco so she wasn't out of pocket.

See that Paris Milton? She's a pure pain in the arse, man. She says it's sick to make jokes about the pure dead, man, but ma Darius and ma Britney are such caring weans that they wrote down all their jokes for us. They want to get as much money as they can for Bern's ma, especially as she'll have to stop claiming his buroo money in a few months when the social catch up with her.

A ned couple were celebrating their fifteenth wedding anniversary with their children and grandchildren at a local pub before they decided to sneak off home for some rampant sex. Unfortunately the husband died but his penis stayed hard, so much so that his wife had to give the undertakers permission to cut it off and leave it in the house to get the coffin lid on. The next day she was alone at the funeral parlour talking to her dead husband, but before she left she decided to stick the severed penis up his arse. Noticing a change in his facial expression she sneered, 'Ah told you it wasn't pleasant, you selfish bastard.'

A keen Hibs fan is sitting all alone, with an empty seat next to him. It's the only empty seat in the ground.

'Who's sitting there, man?' asks a Hibs fan on the other side of him.

'It's ma wife's seat, man.'

'Why's she no here?'

'She's deid!'

'Why did you no' gie her ticket to one of your pals?'

'They're all at the funeral.'

A ned died pure poor and many local shops donated money to the fund for his funeral out of sympathy. The manager of the jeweller's was asked to donate a fiver.

'Only a fiver?' he asked. 'Only a fiver to bury Brad-Pitt Mackenzie? Here's a cheque. Go and bury one hundred of them.'

Malkie was digging the garden when three hearses drove by, huge flower displays all over them, saying 'MUM' and 'GRAN'. They were followed by a line of 200 neds and then an eighteen-year-old ned on foot with a pit bull. Malkie walked up to the man and called out to him.

'Haw, man, who's in the hearse?'

'Aw, man. It's ma burd – the wife.'

'Aw, that's terrible, man. Whit happened?'

'The dug bit her and she died.'

Raised in Pilrig

'Who's in the second hearse, man?'

'Ma mother-in-law.'

'Oh aye. What happpened to her?'

'Dug bit her an' all,' the ned replied.

Malkie considered this for a moment, then said, 'Can Ah borrow your dug?'

'Get in line,' said the ned.

What's the difference between a ned
wedding and a ned funeral?
There's one less drunk at a ned funeral.

At the wake for Brandon, a ned who was always in trouble with the law, a silence fell over the group.

'He was a good boy sometimes. Can one of his pals say something nice about Brandon please?' his mother said.

The hush continued. People shuffled their feet and someone coughed in the silence.

At last, one of his pals muttered, 'His sister was worse.'

Where do you find a good loan shark?
In a graveyard.

After twenty-five years of sticking together in ned marriage, Jimmy is lying on his deathbed at the local hospital. With a tear in his eye he says, 'Joyce, before Ah die, Ah have to tell you something.'

She replies, 'Yes, dear. Whit is it?'

Jimmy starts, 'The first year we were together, Ah caught hepatitis B and almost died. You sat by ma bed and nursed me back to health.'

Joyce nods her head and wipes away a tear, 'Aye, that was pure terrible.'

'And then, when Ah lost my son Kray and his dug Tyson in that terrible hit and run (except they came back for the dug and nicked him), it was you by ma side who kept me going. And when oor daughter Nicollette ran away from hame and took drugs and became a prossie, you sat with me and comforted me. And when Ah lost everything when the hoose burned down, you stood by me. Right to the last, Joyce, you've been through everything with me.' Joyce nods her head, tears streaming down her face.

'Aye, well,' Jimmy says. 'So before Ah die, Ah just want you to know you're a fuckin' jinx.'

What's long, thin and smells of piss?
A ned funeral cortege.

Brenda is distraught at her husband's funeral and has to be dragged off his coffin at the graveyard, screaming. Her best pal takes her to one side and consoles her, telling her that although things seem crap at the moment she still has a future and might even meet a new man in six or seven months' time. 'Six fuckin' months? Ah'll no last til the weekend withoot getting ma hole, man!'

5

Ned Pets
by Keanu

Pets, man, more trouble than weans. We all went off to the graveyard, man, to lay the flowers on Bern's grave, but we could only fit Rage, one of the pit bulls, into the boot, so we left Beckham, the other pit bull, tied up in the front garden. We were all pure, pure devastated. That scaffolding is lethal, man. Bern's ma is going to get Legal Aid to take that construction lot to court.

We came back hame tae find Beckham pure stabbed through the heart, man. He was lying on the monoblock in a pure red pool of blood. Britney was pure hysterical at the shock, man, and went straight intae labour. That dog was the apple of her eye – she used to call him 'Beckham Babe'.

Who killed Beckham? We think it was Wayne and Colette. That Colette thinks she's a pure supermodel and acts like a pure diva cos she's got blonde hair extentions and runs a nail bar but she's pure white trash, man. She turns oor stomachs. Total neighbours from hell, man, pure jealous of oor motors and lifestyle. Darius wanted to put his pet rats, Jordan and Jodie, through their letter-box to pure sort them out but Britney stopped him just in time.

That Colette would've pure shat hersel' if she'd seen Jordan or Jodie but rats are clean pets. This is oor sixth pair – they don't live that long, but we pure look after them and keep them in a cage next tae the microwave cos the kitchen's warm. We used to keep them in the weans' room but they nearly chewed through the cot bars.

Before Beckham got stabbed, Keanu had been planning to mate him with a Great Dane, Coleen, in the next street and spend the money from the pups on the Corsa. Beckham was always sniffing round Coleen. He was gaggin' for her. It was pure obscene, man!

Keanu got some knocked-off colour-coded bumpers and a spoiler but they didn't work out as planned so he's pure forced to buy them now and he's not a happy chappy, man. The neon lighting, sound system and blacked-out windows are all basics but he's pure broke. No accessories and only one pit bull. But oor Darius works down the pet shop, man, and he's going to get another pit bull puppy for us when the time is right. He got these jokes in the meantime and we had a wee wake for Beckham and he told them there, to raise a few laughs. The bevvy was pure flowing and we took it in turns to sup a 'home-brew' from his bowl to toast his departure. Gone but not forgotten.

It's an early Friday evening and two neds, Kelvin and Melvin, are walking down the road with Kelvin's pit bull. A pack of eighty neds are standing in Glenrothes High Street, stopping the traffic and making a nuisance of themselves.

The pit bull's been in a terrible fight and is barely recognisable as a dog any more. The pack of neds see Kelvin and Melvin and the barely-recognisable-as-a-dog pit bull and start on them.

'Haw, man! Your dog's got no nose! How does he smell?'

And Kelvin shouts: 'Haw, man, terrible.'

> What's the difference between a dead ned
> lying at the side of the A8 and a dead dog
> lying at the side of the A8?
> Skid marks across the road, in front of the dog.

A ned walks into the DSS office and shouts, 'Who's the bam wi' the Great Dane tied tae the lamp post ootside?' An old man approaches and says that the dog is his only companion and is indeed his.

The ned says, 'Well sorry tae tell ye, man, but yer dug's deid – ma granny's dug just killed it.'

The old man is shocked and says, 'But my dog is huge, are you sure he's dead?'

'Aye, man, he's just choked on a Yorkie.'

Little Troy has a dog called Duke but the dog is unwell and likely to die within weeks. His dad explains that Duke is unwell, that he's old and had a good life but is likely to

See ma puppy, man? He's gonnae be the star of the new Disney film *Rambo Come Home*. Hawwwwww!

die very soon. Troy is convinced by this and asks if they can have a funeral for Duke.

'Aye, nae bother,' says his dad.

'Can Ah invite all ma pals from school and have cake and jelly and ice cream?' says Troy, kicking the arse out of it.

'Of course you can – you can have all the cakes and jelly and ice cream you want,' says his dad.

'Well, can we kill Duke today, dad?' says little Troy.

After years of arguing and fighting, Bronwen and Ned decide to divorce and go their separate ways. Ned is staying in the marital home so, as Bronwen is leaving for the last time, she opens the fridge and gives the family Rottweiler a large steak.

'Whit ye dae that fur?' says Ned. 'That was ma tea the night.'

'That's for all the help he's given me cleaning the dishes over the years,' replies Bronwen.

Dean is walking down the road with Jasper, his pit bull, when a Punto launches on to the pavement and kills the dog stone dead.

'Haw, man!' shouts Dean, grabbing the dog into his arms and running as fast as he can to the vet on the corner.

'Let us in, let us in!' he shouts. 'Gonnae help me save Jasper, man?'

The vet lifts the pit bull on to the table and examines him. 'I'm so sorry, Mr McClutcheon, the dog is dead.'

'Aw, man, no! Not deid! Are you sure, man? Is there no' some other test you can dae oan him, man? Ah thought you were clever, man.'

The vet considers for a moment and then says, 'Well, there are two other tests we can do but they are expensive.'

'Money's no object, man!' Dean insists.

So the vet brings in a tiny tabby cat. It jumps on to the table and walks its length, surveying the pit bull. The tiny cat sniffs the pit bull, shakes its head and jumps down and walks away with its tail in the air.

Then the vet nurse brings in a Golden Labrador, which pads over to the table where the pit bull is lying, sniffs it and turns to look at the vet. He shakes his head twice and turns mournfully away.

'What was that?' demands the ned.

'It's new techology,' advises the vet. 'We use new techniques to verify our findings.'

'Oh aye, and how much for that, man?' asked Dean.

'Well it's sixty pounds for my time and then there's a total of three hundred for the rest.'

'What's the rest?' asks Dean.

'One hundred and twenty for the cat scan and one hundred and twenty for the lab report.'

There were three pit bulls in the waiting room of the vet's surgery in Easterhouse.

The first pit bull says, 'Ah was out with my owner when he was jumped by a gang and Ah savaged one of them so Ah'm here to be put to sleep.'

The second pit bull says, 'A couple of thieving bastards broke into oor house and stole some of the gear that my owner has taken years to steal himself so, cos Ah bit them, Ah'm here to be put to sleep.'

The third pit bull said he was wandering about the house when he saw his owner's burd bent over naked in the bathroom so he took her from behind. The other two chuckled and said that at least he'd had some fun before he was getting put to sleep.

'Put to sleep?' said the third pit bull. 'Oh no, man, Ah'm only here to have ma nails clipped.'

What do you call a ned with a pit
bull under each arm?
A pimp.

What's the difference between a new
ned boyfriend and a pit bull?
The dog is still excited to see you after a week.

Why do Highland neds prefer
kilts to trackie bottoms?
The sheep find the kilts keep
them warmer during sex.

A ned takes his pit bull to the vet's with his burd. The vet picks the dog up and puts it on the table.

'My,' he says, 'this is a fit-looking dog.'

'Aye, man,' says the ned.

'All this dog needs,' the vet says, having examined him, 'is a few jags.'

'Nae bother,' says the ned.

'You know,' says the vet, 'if your pit bull was a human, he'd be like Linford Christie,'

'Whit?' says the ned burd. 'Big baws?'

What's the difference between a ned and a rat?
Nothing, they both go for the jugular.

What's the difference between
a pit bull and a nedette?
Nothing. They're both dogs, would sniff
your crotch and dry hump your leg.

What's the difference between a husky and a ned?
Nothing. They both move in packs
and pish in the street.

6

Ned Pastimes, Holidays and Employment
by Kylie

Britney was pure happy slapped last week outside the chippy wi' her pals. But she didn't tell me because it was a pure riddie. Ah only know cos it was Paris Milton's niece Destiny that did it and her pal Taramisu took the photae on her moby, man. Taramisu sent the photae to all her mates, plus to Britney. They're slapping an ASBO on Taramisu and Destiny now and Paris Milton is in a fuckin' rage, man. But, see me, Ah cannae help it, man, cos this happy slapping is a national outrage, by the way, and the sooner Tony Blair outlaws that, man, the better.

Ma holiday this year with Keanu was pure quality and you can read about that in the next chapter. Ah left Britney in charge of the weans and me and him went to Florida, man. Ah felt a bit guilty as Britney had only just given birth to the twins – Jordan and Tony-Curtis Pilrig – three days earlier but, hey, who would knock back a holiday?

. . . and now a few words from Paris Milton's niece, Destiny

It's no' fair, right. Ah've got an ASBO slapped oan me now because Ah pure slapped ma auntie's pal's daughter. That Britney pure deserved it. Have you seen the state of her? She was standing about pure posing, like the wee cow she is, outside the chippy and she'd only had twins two days before. It's not just that, right – she was pure flirting with my boyfriend Nico. She's a pure manky bastard, by the way – just given birth and she's standing about with her tits hanging oot and a flabby belly and she thinks she's pure attractive, man. Ma Nico said he wouldn't touch her with his grandpa's but she pure deserved the slap, wee boot.

Hope you like the jokes in this chapter. Cos Ah'm restricted to where Ah can go and stuff, it means Ah've got pure hundreds of spare time so me and Taramisu wrote down all oor jokes for my Auntie Paris. Only thing is, right, Ah didn't realise she was passing them on to that Kylie so she can get money for a bigger pair of diddies.

A door-to-door salesman talks himself into a nedette's house in Possil. He is trying to sell a super-duper high-powered vacuum cleaner. He tips a bag of dust, dirt and filth all over her living-room carpet.

'Whit the fuck d'you think you're doing?' she demands.

'Don't worry, hen. The vacuum will certainly clean up this lot – you'll be amazed. If it doesn't, I'll eat it up myself.'

'Aye,' she replies. 'Ah'm oot of power cards until next Monday, so will Ah get you the ketchup the noo then, you daft bastard?'

Did you hear about the ned granny who took her telly to Gran Canaria so she could watch *Coronation Street*?

There's a new microwave on the market aimed at neds.

It only has five buttons which read: popcorn; boil water; frozen dinner; pizza reheat; frozen chips.

A teenage lad was being told off by his father for spending all day watching daytime telly, drinking Super with his mates and signing on. The father complained that he should now get a paid job, settle down and live the life of Reilly. And the ned said, 'Aye, but Ah dae that the noo.'

A ned is feeling a little unwell after the initial shock of being offered a job with the council. The doctor he goes to see is unaware of the stress that the ned is under due to impending full-time employment and decides to run a series of tests. The blood tests are clear so he asks if he can bring in samples of faeces, urine and sperm.

The ned replies, 'Aye nae bother, doc, I'll just leave ma boxers wi' ye the noo.'

A ned couple were sitting in their high-rise in Sighthill with no money, so the boyfriend suggests she goes out for the night and sells her body. The nedette was dubious at first but was persuaded within three minutes. So at 8 p.m. she left their hovel and returned seven hours later with £4.20.

'Where'd you get the 20p from?' demanded the boyfriend.

'Everyone,' she replied.

How can you tell if a ned has been in your garden?
Your wheelie bin is empty and
your dog is pregnant.

What has four hooves, a tail and an arsehole
in the middle of it's back?
A Clydesdale being ridden by a ned.

A nedette gets a job with easyJet and works her way up the ranks at Edinburgh Airport. Unbelievably, she wins the title of employee of the month and moves on to Continental Airlines where she is deemed to be good enough to work on the Privileged Customer desk.

One day her patience is tested when an anxious and rude customer arrives at the back of a line of first-class passengers. He shoves his way to the front, pushing in before several other passengers who have waited patiently in line for some time.

'Lady!' the impatient passenger shouts. 'I need to get on this plane now!'

'Ah'm afraid you'll have to wait in line like everyone else, sir,' the nedette says.

'Don't you fuckin' know who I am?'

The nedette gives him her best stony stare and takes his hand and holds it up to the rest of the queue, 'This passenger doesn't know who he is, ladies and gentleman.'

The queue titters.

'And fuck you!' the impatient passenger shouts.

The nedette smiles at the thought and is more than a match for this very important businessman. 'Ah'll finish at six,' she declares calmly. 'But you'll have to get in line for that, too.'

Two neds saved up the buroo money and went on holiday to Paris by coach. Then they walked around looking at everything, their baseball caps pushed far back so they could take in the views. They were walking past Notre Dame when they realised the caretaker was calling to them.

'Excuse me,' he said. 'I am in need of some assistance!'

'Haw!' cried Chesney. 'Whit is it, Minister, mister?'

'My bell ringer hasn't turned up and it's almost vespers. I need to ring the bell and can't do it on my own.'

Chesney looked at Scott and laughed, 'Bell ringing! You're jokin', man! Us?'

'I can pay you!' said the caretaker.

'Now you're talkin', man!' Scott said. 'C'mon Chesney. Quality! Bevvy dosh.'

So the two neds followed the caretaker into the bell tower and began the slow climb up the bell tower's many steps.

'This is it,' the caretaker said. 'But there's no time to practise. You pull like this,' he demonstrated, 'and swing the bells like this.' He showed them again.

Chesney brayed loudly, 'Haw, nae bother, big yin, for the two bhoys from the Dear Green Place.'

So Chesney and Scott, with all their might, began to swing on the ropes and soon they had the great bells of Notre Dame ringing clear and true across Paris. However, they hadn't realised quite how exhausting the procedure would be, for soon they were knackered and Chesney had trouble holding on to the rope. Scott was in the same predicament.

'Awwwww nawwwww, man, it's pure slippin'. Ah'm losing it, by the way,' he gasped.

And no sooner had he breathed the words, than the huge bell crashed against him and hit him full in the face.

'Hawwwwwwwwwwww!' screamed Scott as he reeled backwards.

The noise attracted visitors below and they looked up to see Scott, blue and bruised and holding his head and Chesney quickly following suit. The two neds staggered around the tower and stumbled down the stairs, falling and slipping.

It just so happened that the Chief of Strathclyde Police was in Paris for a conference on crowd control at football matches and was on a wee jolly to Notre Dame that evening.

The caretaker came rushing up to check on the commotion and the Chief of Police gasped as he looked at the boys' trackie tops and baseball caps.

The caretaker turned to the Chief of Police. 'Do you know these boys?' he asked.

'Well, I'm not too sure about their trackie tops,' he pondered as Chesney stumbled past, holding his face as blood poured from it, 'but the face rings a bell.'

(Hawwwwwww! Pure corn, man!)

Eight neds get on to a First Bus in Edinburgh and push their way up to the top deck and to the back of the bus. As they weave their way down the bus, they make a racket – barfing, spitting, shouting and finally falling on top of each other as they sit down in the back seats. An old lady sitting just in front of them turns round to shout at them.

Wee Fraser, thirteen, breathes pure Buckie all over her and she turns to look at him with disgust.

'See you, ye wee hooligan in your hoodie and cap?' she calls.

'Aye, man, whit is it?'

'You're goin' straight tae hell!"

'Christ, man! We wanted to go to Gorebridge . . .' shouts Fraser. 'We're all oan the wrang bus!'

What do a ned and a sperm
have in common?
They both have a one in four million
chance of becoming a human being.

Why did the pit bull cross the road?
It had its penis stuck in the chicken.

Why did the ned cross the road?
He had his penis stuck in the pit bull.

Why did the nedette cross the road?
She had her hand in the
ned's poke of chips.

A white horse walks into a bar in Clydebank, where Stevie's working as the relief barman. Stevie is more than a little surprised.

'Haw, big horse,' he says, 'are you lost?'

'Nah,' says the horse. 'A pint of eighty shilling, please.'

'Haw! Big horse!' Stevie exclaims. 'You can talk!'

'Aye, man, nae bother,' says the horse. 'Whit's so special about that?'

'Well,' says Stevie. 'Ah'm from the city, man, so Ah'm no' really used to country stuff, but horses don't usually come into bars, dae they?'

'Nah, man,' says the horse, watching Stevie pour eighty shilling into the pint glass. 'But Ah just fancied a pint.'

'Aye, man, Ah know what you mean,' says Stevie as he hands over the pint.

The white horse shrugs. 'That's magic, thanks,' the horse says.

'Is it the décor, man?'

'Pardon?' says the horse, sipping at his beer.

'The brass on the walls, man – is that what attracts you? Or is it the name? The White Horse Bar of Clydebank. See, man, we don't often get a talking horse in here.'

The horse has to hand it to Stevie. He's very friendly for a relief barman.

'Ah, man, Ah'm just in for a quiet drink. Ah don't like these loud bars with all the noise and food these days, man.'

'I know what you mean, man,' says Stevie, cleaning some glasses and looking up at the bar and the shining rows of bottles there. There is a silence, as the horse drinks his pint reflectively and Stevie struggles for conversation with the talking white horse. His eye falls on a large brown bottle, up with the malts.

'Haw, man!' Stevie exclaims suddenly, nearly dropping his tea towel. 'I don't know how often you go into bars, man, but do you know they named a drink after you, man. A whisky!'

'Really?' exclaimed the white horse. 'Fancy that! A whisky called Ned!'

A family of four neds wins the dream holiday of a lifetime through the *Tricia Show*. It's an all-expenses-paid cruise across the Atlantic, with a flight back to Glasgow from New York City. They can't wait and are very excited about the drink-as-much-as-you-can deal on the five-day crossing and the in-cruise entertainment.

On their first night on board, the magician they meet, who wears a top hat and tails and stoats around the deck with a parrot on his shoulder, bemuses them. Little Tinnifer, aged ten, follows the magician one afternoon, when the rest of the family are up on deck in their recently 'purchased' pristine-white shell suits, and watches him trying to get the parrot to shut up when he is doing his tricks. The magician hides a rabbit in his hat and the parrot shouts, 'It's up his trouser leg!' Or 'It's up his sleeve!' Little Tinnifer asks the magician what is wrong with the parrot and why it's such a squealer.

'Oh, my last parrot died suddenly and I had to go to a pet shop to buy this new one. They told me he was a trained parrot but sadly I think I've been sold a dud.'

'Haw, that's shocking, man,' says little Tinnifer, with deep sympathy. 'Ah wish Ah could help, man.'

The magician thanks him but says he'll have to just make do and little Tinnifer sidles off with his pint to find his da, who is up on the top deck in a brawl. They go to see the magician perform that night and, sure enough, every time the magician does a trick, the parrot squawks, 'It's behind his back!' Or 'It's in his top hat!'

So, as the night wears on and everyone is well sozzled, there suddenly comes a grinding, juddering noise from the bow and the ship starts to sink as the ocean pours in. As it happens, little Tinnifer has had so much to drink, that he's up on deck, throwing up over the side, accompanied by the rest of his family, as the ship goes down. Only the magician, with his parrot, makes it up to the deck in time to jump into a lifeboat with the neds.

So the four neds and the magician and the parrot are bobbing about together on the Atlantic as the ship gasps one last awful breath and sinks down into the waves. The ned mum cries, the nedette daughter is still too sick to comment, the ned dad is nursing his black eye from the earlier scrap and little Tinnifer watches the magician and his parrot with interest.

The magician has spirited up some water and supplies and is watched closely by the parrot. In fact, so close is the parrot's guard that he doesn't even blink. He just sits on the opposite side of the dinghy and stares and stares at the magician. With no wind and no current, the dinghy sits on the spot where the ship sank.

By the second day, in the scorching heat, as they drift on the windless sea, the ned family are all missing alcohol and nursing terrible hangovers. The magician sips water and eats some hard biscuits and soft oranges he's managed to conjure up and is watched by the parrot, who stares like a hawk at him, as the magician chomps merrily away, dressed still in his black tails, hat and shiny shoes.

By the third day, the neds are eating oranges for the first time in their lives and making jokes about eating five pieces of fresh fruit and veg a day while on their holidays. They are still cheerful and smile cos this is still the trip of a lifetime and they've never eaten so healthily. And the magician tells them some jokes and makes them laugh and everyone is getting on quite well, except for the parrot, who sits, eagle-eyed, unsleeping or blinking, staring at the magician.

On the fourth day, with the food supply and water bottles getting low, the magician and neds mostly sleep, bobbing about, unrescued, still on the flat, calm and windless ocean. But still the parrot, unblinking and completely focussed, stares at the magician.

By the fifth day, now certain of death, the neds prepare to meet their Maker, Lonsdale, and simply pray that the end will come quickly. The magician looks up from a long slumber, his bow tie now undone and his top hat slightly squint. His gaze is met by the parrot's.

The parrot, who hasn't blinked in five days, eyeballs the magician. He slowly opens his beak to squawk. They all wait as the parrot moves his head very slightly, to nod briefly at the spot where the luxury liner went down, still in view, and looks back accusingly at the magician. 'OK,' he manages, 'I give up. What have you done with the ship?'

What's the difference between a ned and ET?
ET phoned home.

A ned who has seen the error of his ways gets a job in a local baker's with the help of his probation officer. Each day he tries harder and harder to impress staff and bosses and, by the end of the first week, everyone is amazed at the transformation in him.

The following week, two old ladies come into the shop and ask for two chocolate eclairs and two doughnuts. The ned puts the cakes into a box using a pair of tongs and ties the box with a piece of string. The two women are impressed with his manners and comment on how helpful he's been and also how hygenic it was to use the tongs.

The ned tells the old ladies that he likes to keep his hands clean – hygiene is very important when handling the cakes and that's why he always uses the tongs to pull out his cock and put it back in his trousers every time he goes to the toilet!

A ned lay sprawled across four seats in the Pavilion. When an usher spotted him, he went over and said, 'Excuse me but you can't take up four seats like that.' The ned made a nasal moaning sound and still lay where he was. After several requests to move, the usher was starting to lose patience and threatened to call the manager if the ned still refused to move. He still didn't move and made the same nasal sounds. A minute later, the usher and the manager were standing over the ned, who still lay unmoving and moaning, so finally they call for the police.

The officer in charge says, 'Right, mate, whit's yer name?'

'Connor, man,' replies the ned weakly.

'Where ye from, Connor?'

'The balcony, man.'

Courtney had won the lottery and bought a new penthouse apartment by Ocean Terminal. She was showing a few of her mates around. When they went into the living room, her pal Shannon asked what the huge metal gong and hammer were for. Courtney replied that they acted as a talking clock. Everyone looked puzzled and asked how they worked.

'Here goes,' replied Courtney and whacked the gong with all her strength.

Suddenly there was hammering on the wall from next door and someone shouting, 'Shut the fuck up, it's one in the morning!'

Long-term unemployed Archie runs up the seventeen floors to his council penthouse and announces to his wife that he's just won fifteen million pounds on the lottery.

'Ye're jokin?' Aw that's brilliant. Will Ah pack for the Caribbean or Milan?' his wife coos.

'Ah don't care where you pack for, just get tae fuck,' he replies.

A barman walks up to a ned in a pub and points to a fag end on the floor.

'Oi, mate, is that yours?' he says threateningly.

'Ye're alright, pal, you have it – there's a few drags left in it.'

What's the first question at
a ned quiz night?
Whit the fuck are you lookin' at?

What goes in long, hard and dry and
comes out small, soft and wet?
Ned chewing gum.

A ned walks into a fancy-dress party with his girlfriend, wrapped, piggy-back style, around him.

'Ah've come as a turtle,' he explains.

'Who's that then?' another ned asks, pointing at the nedette.

'That's Michelle,' he says.

A ned is stranded in the desert after his plane to Morocco comes down. Desperate for water, he staggers up a sand dune.

A figure comes towards him, 'Wanna buy a tie?'

'Haw, man, why would Ah want a tie, man? Ah don't even know how to wear a tie, man. Got any watter?'

'Naw, no water, man. Just ties.'

The figure moves off into the distance. The ned staggers on, over the sand dune. He is now really desperate for water. It can only be a few more hours before it's curtains for the ned.

The ned realises he's done in – no water and sand all over his trackie bottoms. He's never felt heat like this before. He's gonna die. He's had enough. He prepares to meet his Maker. Suddenly, another figure appears out of the shimmering haze. The ned feels like he has been saved. He squints at the figure as he looks like he's wearing an Armani suit, out here in the desert, and carrying a briefcase.

'Haw! See me, man? Got any watter?'

The figure with the large pilot bag trots over the sand towards him.

'Wanna buy a tie, man? Louis Vuitton? Paul Smith? Hugo Boss?'

Jist make sure wan ae yous gets a close-up o' ma sovvy ring marks oan his cheek

'Fucksake, man. Got any watter?'

'Nah, man, but these aren't knock-offs. They're the real thing, man.'

'Naw, man. Not for me, man. Ah just wear trackies.'

'Suit yourself, man . . . geddit?' The ned with the ties swaggers off into the heat.

The lost ned slips and slides his way down the sand dune and eyes up another dune, before starting out to climb it. He knows, by his parched throat, that this is his last dune. His short life flashes before him and, in his head, he says goodbye to his ma and pa.

As he clambers to the top of this last dune, he rubs his eyes. He can't believe what he's seeing. There, before him, is the most wonderful sight – an oasis, with a large wall and gate and, beyond, waterfalls and greenery and the constant rushing, gushing, thunderous noise of fresh water. The ned can't believe his luck and musters his last ounce of strength as he totters down the sand dune and arrives at the solid gates of the oasis. On the door is a bouncer, who looks the ned in the eye and then up and down.

'Haw! Big man! Let us in!'

The bouncer stares down at the ned, who is, by now, on all fours.

'You're the answer to my prayers, big yin!' the ned cries.

But the bouncer draws himself up to his full height and stares down at the ned.

'Sorry, pal,' the bouncer says. 'This is a tie-only establishment.'

Tyler, a ned with aspirations of one day living the life of a celebrity featured in *Hello* magazine, wins the trip of a lifetime. He's so excited he packs for a week and when the day comes he's at Glasgow Airport with three hours to spare. So he's on the plane, having a great time, when the plane crashes.

Tyler manages to cling to a passing piece of driftwood and finds himself on a desert island. Four years pass and still he dreams of a life in Spain or visiting resorts such as Benalmadena. One day, out of the sea, comes this beautiful woman in a wet suit. She bounds up the beach and stops in front of him. He can't believe his eyes.

'Hi,' she calls. 'I'm here to rescue you!'

'Haw, man! Ya beauty!'

'But, before I do that, I can grant you three wishes!'

Without hesitation the ned asks for three pints of Stella. The blonde slightly unzips her wet suit and pulls out three pints of Stella. They are ice-cold and Tyler grabs them and guzzles them down in the heat.

'You have two more wishes,' she coos.

'Haw, man! Do you have a fag end, man?'

'I can do better than that,' she says huskily and gives him a Kensitas Club.

'And for your third wish?' the blonde says, with her finger on her full-length body zip.

The ned frowns and thinks.

'You dinnae have a telly with *Tricia* on it, do ya?'

The blonde is a little put out and pouts provocatively.

'Wouldn't you like to play around?' she sighs at Tyler.

'Haw, man!' the ned shouts, triumphantly. 'Dinnae tell me you've got a set of golf clubs in there as well?'

What do you call a ned in a
higher education college?
A visitor.

Two neds walk into a pub.

'Haw, man! So you're no' going tae Venice this year, man?'

'Naw, man. It's Paris we're no' going to this year, man. It was Venice we didnae go tae last year.'

Kevin and Celeste saved up all their benefits for six months and decided to splash out on a holiday to Florida. After seven days in their element in Orlando's theme parks, they head south in their sporty convertible hire car and stop off at the Everglades for a tour. As the boat moves slowly through the swamplands, they spot a crocodile with a man's head sticking out of the mouth. Kevin looks at Celeste and says, 'Flash bastard, we'll need tae get one of they Lacoste sleeping bags next time we're at Braeheid.'

Scottie Adair, Scotland's equivalent to Texas's Red Adair, is called to Iraq to put out the fires in the oil wells. Scottie turns up, having shipped in his green goddess fire engines and six teams of crack neds, who have been trained on a youth scheme. They turn up at a colossal fire – oil blazing everywhere – and the fire engines scream into the heart of the blaze. No one can believe it. Locals gasp as the green fire engines drive into the flames – nee-naw, nee-naw, nee-naw.

The engines finally stop in the white blaze and six teams, each with thirty neds, pour from the packed fire engines and start to put the blaze out with their feet. Stamp, stamp, stamp they go. Soon the blaze, incredibly, is out. An official turns to Scottie Adair and gives him a huge cheque. A local sidles up to him and says, 'What do you think you'll spend the money on Scottie?'

'Ah'll be getting those fuckin' brakes fixed on those damn engines!' Scottie replies.

A ned goes to the doctor about his drinking.

'Ah'm drinkin' too much, doctor. Ah keep drinkin' that Red Bull and cider, man. It makes ma shite black.'

'You'll have to cut your drinking down,' the doctor says.

'Ah, no, doc. The burd'll make me stay in every night, man.'

The doctor thought for a moment. 'Tell her you're suffering from syncopation. That will satisfy her doubts.'

The ned went home and told his partner what the doctor said.

'Whit's syncopation when it's at hame, then?' his burd said.

'I dunno but that's what he said, man.'

When the ned went out, his burd rang her mate to look it up on the internet at work. Her mate looked it up in Google and read, 'Syncopation: irregular movement from bar to bar.'

A ned from Irvine goes to Monklands, Lanarkshire, on holiday and walks into a butcher's and buys a sausage roll. He starts to eat it and suddenly chokes. He walks back into the shop.

'Haw, man! This sausage roll is pure mince, man. Ah mean, it isn't, man. One hauf is sausage and the other is bread.'

The butcher puts down his cleaver and stares at the ned and says, 'Aye well, in these hard times, it's difficult to make both ends meat!'

Two neds are talking over the rehab five-asides. They are both very thin and undernourished and both play as goalkeepers.

'See me, man? Ah always took harder goals than you.'

'No way, man. Ah always took harder shots at goal than you.'

'Right, well, Ah remember in that semifinal when their centre forward took the spot kick and the ball hit me full-oan.'

'Whit happened?' asked the other.

'I had to pay at the turnstile to get back intae the ground.'

A ned grandad has taken up a new pastime in Glasgow. He limps into the bar afterwards and eases himself into a chair.

'Ah'm a little stiff from bowling,' he says, by way of explanation.

'We don't mind where you come frae, sir. What can Ah get you?'

A ned grandad comes out of the pub into a terrible gale. He staggers down the road, clinging to a lamp-post in the wind. The polis come by and stop the car to check he's OK.

'Why don't you go into your house and get out of the storm?' they shout.

'Schssstorm? Schstorm?' came the reply. 'The wife's waiting for me in there and you call this a schstorm.'

It was a very hot summer afternoon and Tam was lying sunbathing naked in the back garden.

'Don't just lie there, get up and cut the grass,' moaned his wife.

'Ah cannae,' he replied. 'What would the neighbours say if Ah cut the grass bollock naked?'

'Well, they'd know for sure that Ah'd only married you for the disability car and attendance allowance.'

Fact! Two ned weans, aged around ten, are talking in Braehead Shopping Centre in Glasgow. The wee girl isn't impressed by the story the boy's telling her so she turns to him and says, 'You talk so much pish, ma fanny's getting jealous.'

How do you make two neds cross?
Nail them both together.

A drunken nedette wanders into a library and says, 'Eh, right, gie me a burger, large chips and a diet coke, hen.'

The librarian is appalled and points out that it's a library.

'Aright,' whispers the nedette, 'gie me a burger, large chips and a diet coke.'

Two neds were barrelling down Fountainbridge, towards the brewery. Kevin saw the lights of the brewery and said,

'Haw, man! It's so good to know that, however much we put away, man, they're always making more.'

'Aye but no' but, man,' his pal said. 'They're workin' nights to keep up now.'

'Where d'you go for your holidays, man?' Tracey asked Sharon.

'Magaluf, man.'

'Pure dead brilliant, man. Where's that?'

'Dunno, man. We fuckin' flew.'

How do you get a ned to climb on to the roof?
Tell him the Buckie's on the house.

Two neds walk into a bar in Glasgow, one after another, sit down side by side and order two Special Brews and two packets of Walkers. They each order two more and then two pints of Strongbow each. Then they start to chat.

'Where are you frae?'

'Fountainbridge, man.'

'That's amazing. So Ah'm Ah.'

They each buy a drink for the other.

'Whereaboots in Fountainbridge, man?'

'Haw, near that UGC, man.'

'Naw, man! That's pure mental. Ah'm frae there!'

'Naw, man! Whereaboots?'

'Munro Terrace.'

'Me too, man. Let me get you another drink. Ah grew up on Munro Terrace.'

'Naw, man! Fancy us meeting up, man, after all these years in Glasgow.'

Just then a regular came in and went up to the bar.

'All right, Davie?' he said to the barman.

'Och, aye, same as usual. The landlord won't gie us Saturday night aff, the burd's giving me jip and the McDaid twins are fleein' again.'

What does a postcard from a ned on holiday say?
'Having a great time but where the fuck am I?'

Declan and Martina are walking along Irvine beach in white shell suits, dragging little Avalon along on a rope behind them, twenty feet out in the sea. A priest walking towards them on the sand stops to admire their heroic attempts to save Avalon from the big waves. He rushes over to see if he can offer any help to rescue her and give last rites but they assure him that everything is under control. As he goes off up the beach, Declan gives the rope a tug and says, 'That dobber doesnae know the first thing about fishing for sharks and diving for treasure, man.'

Jesus walks into a pub in Craigmillar and approaches three neds sitting in the corner, drinking pints of cider. He goes up to the table and says to the first ned, 'Good day to you, young man. You look bothered. Can I help?'

'See me, man? It's ma eyes. Ah cannae focus on ma pint and it's only ma first.'

Jesus touches the ned, who suddenly has twenty–twenty vision and runs outside to tell all his mates congregated at the Spar shop on the corner. The next ned never heard Jesus's question so Jesus touches his ears and suddenly the ned has restored hearing.

Jesus smiles at the third ned but, before he can move towards him, the ned is out of his chair shouting, 'Don't fuckin' come near me, man. Ah'm on disability benefit.'

A ned comes out of the bus station in Edinburgh and walks up to a posh middle-aged woman as she leaves Gucci en route to Harvey Nichols. 'Excuse me, hen. Can you spare a pound? Ah havenae eaten anything for three days.'

The well-to-do lady looks at him and says, 'God! I wish I had your willpower.'

Most neds prefer not to hear their burds struggling with cleaning up the tinnies – so they turn up the volume on the telly.

A ned goes to the doctor and says, 'Doc, see me? Ah cannae stop stealing. Ah'm a pure klepto.'

The doctor prescribes tablets and says that they should help but to come back in a week.

The ned comes back in a week and says, 'Doc, Ah'm still stealing. Ah cannae stop it.'

And the doctor says, 'In that case, next week, come back and bring me a DVD player and an iPod.'

Charlene has all her mates round for an Ann Summers party. She complains at the end of the night to her mate Clio that her new man, Dale, was losing interest after their first week together and nothing she'd seen so far on show that night would push the right buttons.

Clio said, 'Nae bother, Ah've got just the thing in the car. Ah've only got one pair left, in a size twenty-four, they should fit you like a glove. They're crotchless panties, better than a g-string – they're the dog's bollocks.'

So Clio goes out to her Clio, opens the boot and brings back this pair of pure red latex crotchless panties and Charlene is delighted. Everyone goes home and Charlene gets ready for her man, Dale, coming back to the flat. She's lying seductively on the settee wearing nothing but the panties as he comes through the door. He looks at her horrified and she says, 'Do you like what you see?'

And he says, 'Fuck no! Whatever it is, it's started to melt your underwear.'

What do you call a ned in a job centre?
Lost.

Did you hear about the ned who got a job in a pet shop?

He was so ugly that, when other neds came into buy a pit bull, they kept asking how big he'd grow.

Three nedettes, gran, mother and daughter, were reminiscing about their days as prostitutes. A few years previously, the daughter had come home early, very upset as she'd only earned £20 for a blow job.

'No way, hen, twenty quid?' shrieked her ma. 'In ma day ye only got a pound.'

'A pound?' shouted the gran. 'When Ah was her age, we were glad to have something hot in oor stomachs.'

Two neds walked into a pub, having a chat about how bad things were. One had just opened up a tanning shop but things were slow. No business – it was a sunny summer, no one wanted a tan.

'I hear you had a bit of a fire at the tanning shop, Dave,' Tony said.

'Shuttit!' said Dave. 'It's tomorrow.'

A young man and a nedette are in the waiting room at a hospital donation centre. The man asks the nedette what she's doing at the hospital and the nedette says, 'Ah'm here to donate blood – they're gonnae gie me a fiver fur it.'

The man is intrigued and tells the nedette that he's there to donate sperm and he gets paid £25. The nedette is amazed at this and, after chatting for a few more minutes, they go their separate ways.

Three months later they meet again in the same waiting room. The man spots the nedette first and says, 'Hello, here to donate blood again?'

The nedette looks at him and shaking her head with her mouth closed says, 'Uhh-uhh.'

Two neds walk into a bar and one says to the other, 'I didnae sleep with ma burd till oor first date, man! Did you?'

And the other ned says, 'Ah dunno – whit's yer burd's name?'

Two youths are in the waiting room of an office block, waiting for an interview, and they have to fill out some IQ questions. One is, 'Four letters, exclusively female, ends in 'UNT'.' Frank, the ned, scratches his head a lot and looks over at another candidate's paper and the answers he's written down.

'Haw, pal!' he calls across. 'See that clue for UNT, man. Whit's the answer?'

'Aunt,' says the posh candidate.

'Oh, man,' says the ned. 'Have you got a rubber?'

A home-improvement contractor was in Morningside, talking over the changes Mrs Windsor was needing to her house to transform it. She said she thought a Farrell and Ball hunting green would be ideal for her reception hall. The home-improvement woman made a note of this and then opened the front door and shouted, 'Green side up!'

In the dining room, Mrs Windsor said she would like a Caribbean sunset red paint on the walls. The home-improvement woman wrote this down, then dashed to the window and shouted, 'Green side up!'

Mrs Windsor was giving her strange looks by this time but they continued into the upstairs front master bed-room, which Mrs Windsor wanted painted a Hawaiian blue. The home-improvement woman wrote this down also and tore to the window threw it open and shouted, 'Green side up!'

'Could you kindly explain why you keep shouting, "Green side up"?' asked Mrs Windsor.

'Certainly,' said the home-improvement woman. 'I have a team of community-service workers helping me out, working on the garden opposite, and they're laying turf.'

A ned called Max got a job in a fancy-dress shop as a part-time assistant for Christmas. On his first day, he took a call from a man who had to go to the works' Christmas ball but needed to discuss his requirements in private because he had a sensitive problem. Max went into the back for some privacy, where he discovered the man was bald and had a wooden leg. So Max said, 'Ah have just the thing for you. I'll courier it to you immediately.'

The man was delighted and with excitement opened the package the following morning. Three minutes later he was back on the phone to Max at the fancy-dress shop. Max was concerned as the man was upset.

'You've sent me a pirate's outfit,' the man cried.

'Yes,' replied Max. 'Ah thought that would be ideal as you can put the hat and patch on your head and the crutch will help disguise your sensitive problem.'

'Listen, son,' said the man. 'Every fancy-dress shop has suggested this to me for the last five years.'

Max apologised and said he had another idea and would courier it that day. The man still had some hope and faith in the ned, so was excited when the courier arrived the next day. He unwrapped the package but was dismayed when he saw the contents. Within two and a half minutes he was again talking to Max.

'A monk's outfit! Do you know how many times I've been sent one of those?' The man was angry now and shouting.

So Max said, 'Haw, sorry, man. What's so bad with that? You can get away with the bald head and the long cloak covers up your leg. Ah'm no' understanding you.'

The man saw red and said, 'Send me something else immediately! Your ad says that you guarantee customer satisfaction.'

So the ned decided to fix this man for good and promised to send him a package urgently by courier. The next day the man opened his package, which was surprisingly small. Within a minute and a half he was back on the phone, shouting at the ned in the fancy-dress shop.

'Just tell me why you have sent me a tin of treacle?'

'Haw!' said the ned. 'Stick that treacle on yer heid and yer wooden leg up your arse and you can go as a toffee apple, ya prick!'

7

Kylie and Keanu in Florida
by Keanu and Kylie

We thought you'd want tae hear about oor trip tae America and that. Me and Kylie won it in a competition, pure quality stuff, man. There's no way Ah'd be spending that sort've cash on a holiday, man. All Ah'm interested in spending the dosh on is the motor but who'd knock back a free holiday to the USA, the land of the pure obese? Ah've never seen so many fat burds in my life, man. Ah was too preoccupied with pulling a burd anyway – well, that's what Ah'm saying anyhow. Kylie pure loved it too. After her exploits on the plane on the way over, she calmed down and now she's thinking that it'd be better if she got her implants done over there. It's all cos she's seen some other burd getting it done on Sky and she fancies the surgeon – pure taped the programme and everything.

If you've never been to Florida we'd pure recommend it. It was all doon tae me that we won the holiday. We were up early one morning, Ah was signing on and Ah was giving her a lift tae college (she's a mature student, man) and there was a competition on that breakfast telly to win a trip to Orlando. There was a motor and hotels included and everything. The question was 'Florida is on which coast of the USA?' Ah said east and Kylie said west so we both phoned and Ah won. Pure magic, man. Ah went pure mental when they read oot ma name on the telly. Ah couldnae stop jumping up and doon and shouting, 'Ya fucking beauty, man!' for days. Ma ma and da were pure green wi' jealousy.

We got picked up in one of they stretch limos that you see the stars arriving at premieres in. The whole street was oot when we left, man, and people were cheering and shouting as we set off. All we were interested in was the mini bar in that motor. That's the first time we've had champagne – normally, we just get Cava for Christmas and special occasions. Noo we've got a taste for the real stuff, that's whit we'll be having fae noo on. Nae mare cheap shit fur the McGlinchys.

Anyways, right, we got to the airport and got oor cases checked in and Ah could tell that the stuck-up lassie at the desk was jealous of us cos we'd got Burberry luggage. Well, it was pure fake but she didnae know that, did she?

Next stop, the bar. Got a couple of pints of cider and lager doon oor necks before the plane journey. It was only 7 a.m. but Ah couldnae believe how busy the bar was already, man. First time I'd had to queue for a drink at that time of the day, by the way. We'd never been further than Spain before so a trip tae America was the dug's baws. Kylie was starting tae get a bit nervous aboot the flight so Ah got her a double voddie too – calm her nerves and that. No sooner had she downed a few doubles than it was time for duty free.

I'd been careful wi' ma giro's over the weeks before we went and she'd just got her grant through fae college. We were totally sorted for cash. The best bit is ma granny's still claiming attendance allowance for ma granda, who died a while back, so she gave us an extra 500 quid each so we were well and truly on oor way! Dead generous ma granny is, she's the best. Ah got fags, whisky, aftershave, a new pair of shades, a digital camera and some sweeties for the plane. Best no' to spend all ma cash at once. Kylie got fags, voddie, perfume, make-up and new designer shades. Then we went next door and got new Rangers tops and caps. Sorted, man – we looked the business going round the theme parks, man.

After a wee while, we got movies and shit on the plane but it was boring so we started tae tan the drinks that they trolley dollies were handing oot. Ah was totally loving that part, man – free swally. We couldnae believe it, man, quality. The only pain in the arse was the amount of weans on the plane. Why were there so many sprogs, man? It's no' like Florida's a place for families and that, eh? The high-light was the couple wi' seven weans but they werenae keeping an eye on them – no way, man, more interested in the free bar like us.

Even when they weans were shouting for their ma and da, they just pure blanked them and carried on drinking till two of their wee boys started fighting and one got his nose burst and the blood was everywhere. That was when the shit pure hit the fan, man. Their ma charged up the aisle and leathered the arse of the innocent one but me and Kylie just kept oot of it. No way were we getting involved in that, man – they looked pure rough. Even the cabin staff were losing the rag wi' them – caused total mayhem, man, and disturbed other passengers and that. Pure tubes the lot of them. The da should've knocked the shit oot them all but Ah think he'd passed oot wi' the swally. Some folk don't know when tae say no, enough's enough, man.

Next thing Kylie was getting a bit of attention fae wan of they male cabin boys. He kept looking at us and smiling but she was too busy reading her magazines. Then Ah realised that it was me, man, no' her that he's staring at! Aw, naw, man, Ah was sure the guy was a bender – he was pure eyeing me up – no fucking way, man. Kylie was pure loving it and ringing the buzzer for him to bring mare drinks. Ah felt totally uncomfortable, man – ma mates would rip the pish oot o' me if Ah got chatted up by a man, man – a man that likes another man, it's no right, man.

By this point, Ah was wishing Ah hadnae changed into my footie top and hat in the airport pish-hoose – Ah knew Ah was looking good dressed like that but Ah wasnae wanting his attention. It didnae help that Kylie was ordering drinks constantly and knocking them back like she was up the social club on a Friday night. I'd just aboot had enough. She was getting totally pished oot her box and she'd been refused any mare drinks, thank fuck, cos she was beginning to piss me right aff wi' her flirting and comments to the pretty boy.

Next thing, she disappeared tae the bogs but she was gone for ages and Ah couldnae see her anywhere. Ah waited a wee bit longer before Ah got someone to look for her, man – it wasnae real. Turned oot she was so pissed that she got talking to a guy that was in the queue for the bog and they were shagging! She wanted to join the fucking Mile High Club while his wife was watching the film! It was beyond fucking belief, man. How the fuck did they both fit intae that wee cubicle thing? And who did that prick think he was, two-timing wi' ma cousin anyway? Ah should've burst him!

When the commotion died doon and Kylie had passed oot in her seat, Ah had tae act like Ah was sleeping fur the last few hours of the journey. Ah was pure embarassed by all they folk looking at us after that guy's wife slapped Kylie right across the coupon – a pure beauty. Kylie was right on form, man – she threw her a right hook right back.

When the plane landed, Ah was pure shocked, man, that me and her were the only two that applauded. It's a tradition, man, that when the plane lands in Alicante everyone cheers and claps. Whit was the matter wi' they people? It was bad enough, man, that we had to fill in cards to get intae a country but we were sitting wi' folk too stuck-up tae clap! After a huge queue to get through they customs at the airport, we got oor luggage – it was easy to spot oors on the conveyor thingy. Everyone was looking at us pure jealous cos we've got designer and they were all waiting like bawbags for identical black cases.

Then oor next stop was car hire. The guy at the desk looked at us like we were aliens or something, man. Ah asked him if he'd ever seen a Rangers tap before but he didnae have a clue, man. He was a pure bam, man. The motors for hire were all displayed on the wall. Ah thought we'd get one of they convertibles and we could drive aboot pure posing like pure film stars. Turned oot that lot aff the telly had only booked us a poxy fucking Cavalier. It didnae even have blacked-out windaes or a max-power stereo! No real, man. Thank fuck ma mates didnae see me driving that – it was a motor for a pure pussy.

Getting the hang of an automatic motor wasnae easy either, man, when Ah'm used to revving up the Punto until it sounds like the engine's gonnae explode before Ah change up a gear. The holiday was starting to piss me right off, man. Kylie was raging as well cos her image didnae go wi' the motor either. We thought the hotel would be like total pure class and that but naw. After a two-hour drive to go ten miles, we got to oor hotel. Ah wasnae sure when Ah saw the ootside – it looked like a Travelodge but it wasnae too bad. No' pure luxury or anything like that but it was clean enough and the wee burd at the reception was pretty fit – wouldn't have minded giving her one over the desk, man.

The first night, we didnae go far in case we got pure lost again in that fucking motor so we went tae Pizza Hut across the road. Ah just had the same as when we go tae Braeheid for shopping and that. Cannae beat the Hut, Ah think – pure magic, man. After the meal, we just headed back tae oor room, man. Long flight and stuff so we were both pure knackered and just pure crashed oot and slept right through tae the next morning. Ah pure dreamt about they all-you-can-eat breakfasts, man. Must've been a good dream cos Ah remember waking up wi' a stonner and thinking shit, hope Kylie hudnae looked over fae her bed and pure clocked it. Big beamer, man.

So, we got ready and headed oot tae wan of they buffets – fill yer boots for $4. Ah mean, where can you get that at hame? Nowhere, man – pure rip-off prices that we pay. After that, we collected oor free theme park tickets and headed tae Disney. Aw, man, that place is pure mental. It's massive. We got on a train thing to take us fae the motor to one of they mental monorail things that take you tae the entrance of the park. Mickey and fuckin' Minnie were standing there waving. Kylie started pure screaming and crying cos she didnae think they were real even though Ah telt her hunners of times that they were.

It was a bit of a riddy cos wee weans were pure scared of us cos of the noise she was making and security took us aside till she was calm and they pulled me up for swearing. Said it wasnae allowed cos it's for weans and families and that and we were scaring people. One of them even said we looked like we could be on *Jerry Springer*. That was quality, man – Ah was pure chuffed wi' that. Jerry is the main man. As far as Ah'm concerned, he's the American Trisha. Ah started tae wonder if we could get on his show while we were there. All the family would have been pure raging cos they never got on it but they'd see us on Sky. Ma da loves that show – he even chants along wi' the audience, 'Jerry, Jerry, Jerry.' Well, Ah'm sure that's what they shout but Ah'm no' too sure though, man.

Kylie calmed doon so we were allowed intae the park. It's like nothing you've ever seen, man. If you think that M&D's at Strathy is big, then this is pure massive, man. The castle is pure huge and there's shops all leading up tae it like olde worlde and stuff. There were cartoon characters all over the shop and weans were waiting to get them to sign bits of paper. Kyles wanted to queue too but Ah thought it was a waste of time, man. Better getting straight to the rides if you ask me. The mention of rides cheered her up – it's her favourite word, man.

Ah was pure bloated after my breakfast, man. Total quality. I'd recommend it tae anyone, man. Anyways, right, we were pure stuffed and decided tae go on Big Thunder Mountain, a rollercoaster set in the Wild West. She was pure busting ma heid to go on it. The waiting time would bust yer arse for a lot of they rides but it was early so we only had tae wait thirty minutes. We had pure trash in the queue next tae us, man. A couple wi' a wean. The wean done a pee against the fake boulders and the husband had a sovvy ring on every finger. Me and Kylie were a bit disgusted – Ah mean how common to let your kid act like that in public. And, as for the rings, less is more. He'd gone too far having all that gold. Nae class, man.

The most scariest bit, man, was when we got on the ride and we were pure screaming and shouting and that was before it even started, man. Ah near shat mysel' as the cars started and it climbed up the first hill. Next thing it's going dead fast and Kylie's Rangers cap fell aff. We were raging, man. That cap wasnae even two days' old and it's fell aff. We should've been warned that caps can come aff oan rollercoasters. So, right, the thing eventually stopped and we demanded that someone climb doon intae the canyon thing and get it back. No fucking way were we for leaving without it, man.

Ah think the guy that worked the ride was scared of us. Next thing the security guards that took us aside at the entrance had arrived on an electric buggy thing and cautioned us about oor behaviour. They wouldnae like it if they lost a baseball cap within two days would they? We got the thing back anyway, after one of them climbed intae the machinery of the ride and got it. By this time, there was a ninety-minute queue and an oil stain on the cap but Ah'm sure Ah'd have been lifted by the sheriff if I'd said fuck all.

We went for something tae drink and had a sit doon cos we were knackered standing about in the sun for pure ages. The rest of the day we wandered about for fuckin' miles, man, just taking it all in. There were queues for all the rides, weans greeting, loads of eating places and cartoon characters stoating aboot on big parades and hunners of fireworks and that. Pure magic but my only complaint was that there wasnae a pub selling Tennents Super. That'd have pure made ma day – a pint of Super, man. Kylie said she'd have liked a pint of that, too. You know, there's thousands and thousands of people everyday in these parks and not one person stopped us tae tell us that they were fae Glesga too or tae take oor photies. Makes me wonder if wearing oor footie gear abroad is worth it. Ah mean, Jack McConnell should be proud of folk like us that pure love oor country and dae hunners tae promote it abroad and that.

Keanu, he never lets me speak, man. So here's a few words fae me aboot America and that. Ah had tae share a room with him. Ah thought that telly company we won it through would know that a burd likes her ain space, man. He's pure wild, man. He takes pure ages getting ready tae go oot – much longer than any burd Ah know. Ah mean, Ah thought ma mate Paris Milton was bad. All he had to do was get on his trackies and trainers, man, and do that shaving thing but Ah caught him using my razor, man. Whit's that all aboot? I'd only used it the once – the night before I'd done ma bikini line – and he was shaving his ugly mug wi' it! So Ah was standing ready and waiting tae go oot, chewing ma gum, man, and Ah said, 'Keanu! Are you ready?' and he's still in the bathroom, man, splashing on pure Paco Rabane and mincing while ma heels were killing me waiting.

I'd pure made an effort and got all dressed up and that. Well, you never know when you might pure bump intae a film star in America, man. So, that started him moaning that Ah was moaning, man. See he disnae shut up. He says Ah don't shut up but Ah cannae get a word in edge-ways. They gied you the breakfast in the deal here but it's

It's good to see that national stereotyping has moved on from the shortbread-tin image of the piper in a kilt

doughnuts and pure carbs, man. Ah cannae eat they things. Ah made him drive us to this diner, man, so Ah could have eggs and bacon. The bacon was a really strange – pure strips they eat with their fingers, man.

They asked you how you want yer eggs every time, man, and gie you twenty different combinations – eggs over easy, eggs sunny side up, scrambled (with twenty yokes, man), poached, boiled, white only, yolk only, low cholesterol, high cholesterol. There were these really dry bagels, man, that Keanu ate but they're as dry as your granny's fanny, man. Ma teacher used to go on about table manners but some of them don't even use a knife and fork there – pure animals, by the way.

Eventually Keanu got himsel' ready and got me to drive, man, cos he's missing the Punto. Said that the hire car was a heap of shite. The car pure reeked of air-freshener. Ah opened all the windaes cos it was fuckin' roasting. Pure nightmare of a drive and we ended up only staying at the beach fur twenty minutes, man, cos Ah lost a nail. Ah couldnae find it in the sand and it was breezy down there. Ah felt sick, too – sand everywhere and Ah had the boak after all they eggs for brekkie.

We went back tae the hotel – it took us nearly two hours each way. Keanu drove back – says Ah'm a wank driver. Ah just pure laid by the pool back at the hotel. Keanu fell asleep, but, so Ah walked out to the beach bar in the middle of the pool.

There was a pure shag of a guy who bought me voddie and cokes, man. Only we got chatting and Ah forgot about

Keanu, man. He got pure burnt by the sun. Ah was back up in the room getting ready tae go out wi' this guy fae the pool, man, and Ah was gagging fur a fag. Ah couldnae find Keanu's jacket anywhere tae knock one of his. Then Ah realised he must have it wi' him and, if he wasnae on the balcony or in the room, he must be at the pool pure burning! So Ah phoned him, man, and texted him but that guy Ah arranged tae meet started texting me, so Ah didnae know what to dae. Ah didnae want to be late for a date, man, but Ah was desperate for a fag. Keanu had all the money, so Ah texted this guy, Damon, back tae let him know Ah was still up fur it, then had to pure put my flip flops back on and go back doon tae the pool tae find Keanu.

He was fast asleep, man, but Ah was so gutted cos he had no fags left that Ah never noticed his skin at first. He'd turned pure red, man. He was pure lobster. Ah was totally devastated for him, man. Ah just pure started screaming, man, and all they pool attendants came running and tae see what had happened. One of them was a pure hunk. Ah wondered about texting Damon back tae delay him just in case something worked out with the pool attendant – his name was Brad.

He did some sort of first aid stuff on Keanu, man, and Ah was like pure melting into Brad's eyes. He was pure muscle, man. He was as muscular as Rage, ma pit bull. So Brad gave Keanu some water and said he'd better lie in a darkened room and Ah thought, 'Well, there goes my night.' Anyway, man, Brad gied ma tits a good look and then stared at me real close. Ah pure knew he thought Ah was top babe material, man, and he said in this dead deep voice, 'See you tomorrow.' Ah got this pure thrill through my spine, man, right up to my hair extensions, and Ah said, 'Right, hunk, see you ra morra.'

Ah was pure rushing aboot cos Ah was gonnae be late, so Ah took Keanu up tae the room. We had to be quick cos Ah wanted to get back down tae see Damon and Ah was looking pure gorgeous, man. Keanu had started to chuck up by then – spew everywhere – and wanted me to get him some water and some after-sun. Ah said, 'OK, aye, see you later.' Ah gied him a quick kiss on the heid and left. Ah felt pure terrible for him, man, but after that it all got a bit hazy.

Ah went for a few swallies wi' Damon and all Ah remember is being in this alley out the back of a club, man. It was pure dead brilliant. Damon said Ah was totally gorgeous, man, and we were like shagging dead sensual and that. Then Ah looked over Damon's shoulder and doon the alley Ah saw Keanu coming oot of one of they all-night chemists, man, carrying a load of bottles. Shit, he'd went and got his ain water and after-sun. Thank god he didnae see me, man. Just as well we were up against the bins, man. Damon wanted to walk me back after. He's a pure romantic. We went via the all-night chemist and Ah bought all this stuff for Keanu and took it back, like. Damon wanted to come up but Ah said Ah was sharing and he was my cousin.

Ah had tae creep in cos Keanu was asleep, man. Ah don't know if he believed me or not about what time Ah went to bed, man – Ah just said he must have been asleep and Ah came in around 2 a.m., not 6 a.m. Ma heid was bursting and ma mouth was like a badger's arse in the morning. Ah had to try and act normal so Keanu believed me and didn't think Ah'd been a dirty wee cow being oot all night, especially when he wasnae well and couldnae get a shag himsel'.

Anyway, Ah got him some brekkie fae the hotel caff and left him to eat that, gied him hunners of water and headed aff down tae the pool wi' ma g-string bikini tae see if Brad was there. Ah hoped tae fuck that Damon was having a lie-in, man. There wasnae any sign of Brad but wi' Keanu no' well Ah knew I'd probably have tae stay aboot the pool for a few days. Plenty of time, Ah thought, tae entice Brad, the babe. The g-string bikini left little tae the imagination so Ah thought Ah'd better warn Keanu about using ma razor again – last thing Ah was wanting was a rash doon there, man! Last time Ah had anything like that, Ah had to go to a clinic, man – pure terrified Ah was gonnae die – but a wee visit tae the sexual health clinic and Ah was sorted, back in action in nae time.

Anyways, Ah was pure bored lying at the pool masel' and ma bikini bottoms were cutting right intae me. Then Ah saw Brad coming towards the pool wi' another burd. He didnae even see me at first and he's like pure flirting wi' this wee slag in a micro bikini. Ah mean Ah could pure nearly see whit she hud for breakfast – cheap wee boot. Then he clocked me looking pure beautiful. Ah sat up on ma sunlounger with my legs wide apart, my feet on the ground on either side it. Ah suppose when Ah think aboot it he might think Ah'm a bit flirty but the pose was unintentional, man. Keanu always sits wi' his legs apart and naebody says fuck all. Right, so he'd clocked me and guess whit? The bastard fuckin' blanked me and walked on wi' the bimbo he was talking to.

Pure big douche-bag, man. Who the fuck did he think he was? If Keanu had been his usual self, he'd have pure kicked him in the baws for that. Ah mean Ah know Ah'd only said hello to him but Ah'd convinced masel' we'd at least have a five-minute chat and a shagathon. Ah mean, man, Ah pure showed aff ma pish-flaps at a pool for him. Paris Milton says Ah probably looked like a cheap whore but Ah think my behaviour was OK – nae different tae chasing guys in a club at weekends.

Ah decided Ah'd better go and see how Keanu was and tell him Ah was pure shattered – Ah'd been blanked by a bawbag in lycra. He wasnae in the room when Ah got back. Ah phoned him and he was in the bar at the reception. Ah thought I'd better cover up so Ah put on a sarong ma ma gied me. Well, it's actually an old duvet cover cut up but it's a pure summery pattern. He was absolutely pished when Ah got there and it was only lunchtime. He looked like a pure dobber, man – bright red wi' blue shorts and a white vest on and he was walking like he'd shat himsel' but Ah suppose it was cos of the sunburn. Well, Ah hoped it was the sunburn!

That was a pure disaster of a day, worst of the whole holiday. Ah'd been blanked, nae sex, he was pished and Ah

was shattered fae being oot all night wi' Damon. Ah
started tae think that mebbes going on an all-expenses-
paid-holiday-of-a-lifetime wasn't all it was made out to be
in the *Daily Ned* and on telly. So I had a double voddie and
coke an' then another, and followed Keanu oot to the
pool. Keanu went to look for a couple of empty sun
loungers. There were plenty with Union Jacks on, man,
reserved for the England fans, so he ended up grabbing
two by the paddling pool. There weren't many weans
anyway, man, so I left him sorting out his towel and I
wandered aff to the bar and Brad started chatting tae us.
He said something about not letting Keanu lie in the sun
again but Ah pure blanked him, man – Ah wasnae having
that. So Keanu laid down and Ah moved one of they sun
umbrellas over so he was pure in the shade. Ah still cannae
believe Ah done this but then Ah kissed Keanu full on the
lips, man, to show that perv Brad that Ah didnae give a
monkey's fuck aboot him. But Keanu was pure snoring by
that time, man, and Brad could see that, so Ah laid down
on top of him and made sure Brad got a pure eyeful of ma
bikini top, man. Ah wouldnae have done it if Keanu was
awake, man. Some of ma pals think Keanu is pure meat,
man, but he's my cousin – now what Ah mean?

Anyway, Ah sat down on a lounger, man, and Ah got
an idea. Ah borrowed some sun cream from this bloke
nearby who was no' bad-looking. Ah gave him a flutter of
the eyelids and blew a wee kiss over my shoulder as Ah
walked away – pure Marilyn Monroe. Brad was still looking, by the way. Anyway, Ah wrote in factor thirty on

Keanu's forehead. First Ah spelt oot 'wanker' but the guy on the next lounger was looking at me so Ah lovingly wiped it off. Then Ah wrote 'Hot Stuff' instead, man – just having a wee giggle tae masel'. I put 'Shag Me' on the back of his hands, man.

Ah sauntered back over to the good-looking guy with the Factor Thirty and gave him his tube back. As Ah did that, he said, 'That your man?' I had tae think fast, man, cos I'd laid on top of Keanu, kissed him and written 'Hot Stuff'on his heid, man, and all, so Ah thought I'd come clean wi' this one.

I said, 'He's ma cousin. Second cousin. But ma display there was for that Brad guy over there.' Factor thirty looked across the pool at Bradley Boy. 'Sorry, Ah know,' Ah said. 'That guy asked me oot on a date and then he stood me up. Ah was just getting ma own back – know what Ah mean? He made me feel like a pure tube.'

'Well,' said Factor Thirty, 'if you really want to get your own back, why don't you and me get a drink.'

I was pure floating, man – thought Ah'd been slipped an E. Heaven. And back. So Factor Thirty and me went over tae the beach bar and had a few voddies and just pure laughed. Ah didn't get a shag, man, which was pure disappointing cos Ah'd only been humped once that holiday. Ah would've liked mare dick but whit's a girl tae dae? Factor Thirty did say he'd see me later in the bar if Ah fancied it. Eh, aye! And he pure gied me his number too.

By the time Ah got back to Keanu, he was pure exposed to the sun again. It was all right really cos he was snoozing in his long-sleeved T-shirt and long trackies, man, so only the words 'Hot Stuff' stood out on his forehead and the 'Shag Me' on his hands, so it wasnae as bad as the day before. His cheeks were redder though, man, and he'd started peeling too. Ah woke him up that time cos Bradley Babe was looking over again. He was like the fuckin' polis, man, that Brad guy. Ah think he was just pure jealous, by the way. There was no way Ah'd have shagged him after that.

Keanu wanted to go oot to buy some jeans. Ah still hadnae waxed but didnae want him going himsel' cos he could barely walk cos of the burns so Ah went wi' him. He'd been doing ma heid in so much Ah was ready to go scripto, man. He drove us tae the factory outlet. Those American outlets are like nothing we have in Scotland, man. They're pure massive and stay open till 10 p.m.

So he went into the first jeans shop, man, and the staff pure stared at us. Keanu had his baseball cap pulled right down over his forehead, man, to cover 'Hot Stuff'. Ah told him some wee girl must have come by and done it while he was sleeping – cos Ah was over at that beach bar again with Factor thirty.

Anyway, that was ma first real blazing row with Keanu. Ah know he was pure stressed. He was in pure pain from his red-raw legs and had these strips over his nose and on his cheeks cos of the sunburn. He had near third-degree burns, man. So Keanu was stood standing, man, looking through the jeans and my feet started hurting. They were pure throbbing. Ah couldnae stand in heels fur longer than five minutes, man.

So Keanu took the pure huff. Said Ah'd been a pure pain in the arse since we'd got there. Said Ah'd been pissed the whole time and he'd looked out for me but Ah'd done nothing for him. And Ah hadnae even looked out for him when the wee girl was writing 'Hot Stuff' and 'Shag Me' on him with the factor thirty or covered him up with that umbrella when the sun moved round.

That was quite interesting, really. Ah hadnae realised the sun would move in the same direction as it did at hame and Ah was pure confused. Ah said Ah thought the sun might have gone the other way, so he would have been covered. He stopped in his tracks for a minute tae think aboot it, then said Ah was pure dead stupid and why didn't Ah use ma fuckin' brain for once.

I started greeting, but that didnae work, so Ah stopped and tried something else – Ah shouted back. That's how we got moved ootside by security. It was pure embarrassing by the way. Then Keanu just pure walked off, man. He went tae the next shop and left me pure standing, wi' all they Americans staring at me. So Ah just pure stomped aff back tae the motor and waited there for him.

He came back eventually, wi' a jeans bag, but Ah had just sat and waited in the heat and fell asleep, man. Ah felt a bit sorry for him then cos he looked pure upset. He still had that tape all over his face and his baseball cap pulled down and his legs were making him walk like Douglas Bader in that *Reach for the Sky* film, man. And Ah thought of ma pals saying he was pure meat, man – like a young George Clooney – so Ah just said sorry and didn't shout any mare.

He said it was alright then didnae speak at all to me, which isnae like him. And then we drove out of the car park but he stalled the piece of shit that the motor was and the barrier came right doon on the bonnet, man. He got a real fright. There was such a bang, Ah thought we'd been shot at. He totally lost it, man. He started pure raging and swearing and Ah thought he was going to cry, he was that upset. The barrier was going boing, boing, boing, boing, boing on the bonnet and he couldnae get the motor started. To make it worse, all they Chevrolet cars were honking at us, trying to get oot, behind us. There were hunners of shoppers totally raging cos of us blocking the way. Tough shit, man. It was oor motor that was getting a hammering.

He did get the motor going, then just pulled away dead fast as the man put the barrier back up. There was a smell of burning rubber and skid marks on the tarmac. It was pure terrible but Ah still had tears running down ma face fae laughing so hard. Then, tae make matters worse, man – sometimes Ah cannae seem tae dae the right thing – Ah took a picture of him. He looked pure grumpy, man, and was growling oot of the front windae. His jaw was down beside his baws, man. And, when Ah took the picture, the flash went aff in his face and Ah really thought he was gonnae crash the motor. He swerved really bad, man. Then he started shouting and swearing again at me, man.

It was pure unnecessary. Mind you, man, everyone in America seems to drive so mental that Ah don't think anyone even noticed. Ah suggested going tae a new theme park the next day that had just opened but he just totally blanked me. He was in a pure shit mood. You'd have thought Ah'd done something pure outrageous.

Ah'm telling you, Ah was pure glad when we got on that plane tae come back hame, man. He spent the last three days no' saying a word tae me. We packed in silence, man, and Ah tried to get him to talk but he pure had the hump, so in the end Ah ignored him, man. He either sat in the room or in the bar – it was a pure wee shame really. Ah went out with Factor Thirty to the new theme park. But it wasnae the same somehow. Ah'm no' sure why. He didnae open doors for me like Keanu did, although I'd never really noticed that before and it made me realise that Keanu was a good guy underneath all the sticking plaster. Ah wasnae gonnae tell him that – Ah hate men that sulk.

We sat in silence on the plane coming back too, man. It was pure annoying. But, on the other hand, they had this new film with Brad Pitt on, so Ah watched that. Ah was pure moist fantasising aboot Brad Pitt and me. Keanu just sat there, trying to sleep, and ignored me. Ah can be a right arsey bitch though, so Ah ignored him back. But Ah behaved masel' and Ah didnae go intae the toilet wi' anyone – even though the guy wi' the Adidas trackie in 69F looked like a right good shag.

8

Ned Children
by Keanu

When Kylie had her latest wean, Abi, she wanted a portrait tae send tae all the family. A lot of them are in the jail and hadn't seen the kid. Wee Abi looked pure beautiful in her pure white furry hat and coat. She looked like the Snow Queen. Her ears had been pierced for the occasion. Wee gold studs and a matching bangle – quality, man.

That's the best age cos any older and they're pure out of control. Paris Milton's daughter is only ten and she's got an ASBO for shooting at passing buses with an airgun and drinking alcohol. She was a pure crazed gun-toting wee bastard and went mental cos she couldn't get 'Ned Barbie' doll. Ah hope that the weans in ma family don't get in with a bad lot.

Anyway, that Abi is a total credit tae oor family. We're so proud of that wean. We were sitting talking the other night, wee carry-oot at oor feet and that, when Abi overheard her ma getting pure upset cos she can't afford her implants just now. You know what it's like, the booze is lapping and you get upset. But anyway, right, that wean went through to the room and came back and pure handed her ma her jewellery that she wore in the Snow Queen photies as a baby and told her tae pawn it and put the cash in her credit union account.

Oor Kylie just burst out greeting and hugged oor Abi for ages. Ah thought she'd go mental when Abi said she wanted to be a glamour model when she's sixteen but Kylie thought it was pure great and special that mother and daughter had the same ambitions. So anyway, the jokes in this chapter are a mix of what we came up with when we were having oor wee bevvy session that night and some are based on oor family experiences. By the way, man, some names have been changed to stop any family feuds.

Little Tatiana, aged three, decided it was time to follow her father's example and start swearing at everyone. So she went downstairs for breakfast and shouted to her ma, 'Ma, Ah'm up! Put out ma fuckin' Frosties.' Her ma was slightly shocked, but not that surprised, so she sent Tatiana back to her room to reconsider her behaviour. She then asked Tatiana's little brother Aaron what he'd like for his breakfast. 'Well, one thing's for sure,' he replied, 'Ah'm not having the fuckin' Frosties.'

A nedette gives birth to a baby that is so ugly the doctors say, 'I'm sorry. We did all we could but he pulled through.'

The ned baby was so ugly his mother refused to breast-feed him. She said she only liked him as a friend.

A nedette gives birth to a baby that's so ugly she has morning sickness after he's born.

I'm not saying that the nedette's baby was ugly but, when he got kidnapped by a rival ned gang and they sent a piece of his finger, she asked them to send more proof.

I'm not saying the ned's kid was ugly but, when he played in the sandpit, the cat kept covering him up.

The ned baby was born so ugly that the doctor slapped the mother.

The ned kid was so ugly he could tell his parents hated him because the bath toys they got him were a toaster and a radio.

The ned teenager was so ugly his mum sent him to join a bridge club.
   He jumps off next Tuesday.

A little nedette, Arlene, aged seven, goes to see Santa. She queues impatiently for a few minutes and then jumps on to his knee.

'Hello, little girl, what's your name and what can Santa get you for Christmas?'

'Haw, Santa,' she cries. 'Ma name's Arlene and can Ah get an iPod, a PowerBook G4, a widescreen telly for ma bedroom, a stereo – Bang and Olufson – and an Eminem extended DVD. Plus ma ma would like a holiday somewhere hot, doesn't matter where, and a date with Brad Pitt.'

The nedette's mother screams over, 'Say please, Arlene, for Christ's sake!'

'Please,' adds little Arlene.

'Well, now,' says Santa. 'That's quite a tall order for my elves and I think the weight might ground my sleigh, ho ho ho! But since you've asked so nicely, are you sure you wouldn't like a doll?'

'A doll, Santa? Well, OK then, if you're short. Whit about a Barbie and a GI Joe?'

'Ahhh,' says Santa, stroking his beard. 'A Barbie doll! Yes, my elves up in Lapland should be able to manage that for you. But, ho ho ho, Arlene, doesn't Barbie come with Ken?'

'Naw, Santa,' replies little Arlene. 'She comes with GI Joe. She fakes it with Ken.'

Little Declan pricked himself with a drawing pin at nursery school and asked the teacher if he could soak it in cider.

'Cider?' asked the teacher 'Why do you want that?'

'Well, ma sister says everytime she gets a prick in her hand she wants it in cider.'

A wee Glasgow woman, called Senga, and a baby were in the doctor's waiting room. When the doctor arrived he examined the baby and found that his weight was below normal.

'Bottle or breastfed?' asked the doctor.

'Breast,' she replied.

'Well, you'd better strip to the waist,' ordered the doctor. She did and he cupped, kneaded, rolled and pinched both breasts for several minutes giving them a thorough examination. He told the patient to get dressed and said, 'No wonder he's underweight, you don't have any milk.'

'Aye, Ah know,' she says, 'Ah'm his gran but Ah'm glad Ah came.'

A squad of builders arrive in Castlemilk to start work on new homes to regenerate the area. Brendan, aged five, starts hanging about the site every day and soon the builders start chatting to him, giving him errands to run and some small jobs on the site. At the end of the first month, they give him an envelope containing £20.

Brendan is made up with this and immediately runs home to his ma who suggests they pay it into her credit union account for 'safekeeping'. At the pay-in desk, Brendan tells the cashier that he earned his money helping to build a house for a month.

'Really? And will you be helping to build it for another month?' asked the teller.

'Aye,' says the lad, 'if the fuckin' bricks ever get delivered.'

Miss Morton was reading ' The Three Little Pigs' to her primary one class. When she came to the part about the first pig gathering material to build his own home she read, 'And the little pig went up to the man with the wheelbarrow full of straw and said, "Pardon me, sir, but can Ah have some of your straw to build my house?"'

'And what do you think the man said?' asked Miss Morton.

Starr raised her hand and said, 'I think he said, "Fuckin' hell, a talking pig!"'

Dougie has just been released fom Saughton Prison after a month and arrives home to see his son on a new mountain bike.

'Where did you get the cash for that?'

'By hiking,' said his son.

'Since when are you into hiking?' asks Dougie.

Ma hobbies? Smokin', drinkin', lightin' fires, goin on the rob . . .
Oh, aye, an' scrappin'

'Well, since you went away Uncle Danny's been round most nights and Ah've been told to take a hike.'

Three young kids are smoking behind Possil Health Centre.

'Ma da blows the best smoke rings,' says the first.

'Ma da blows smoke through his nose and mouth at the same time,' says the second.

'Ma da blows smoke through his arsehole and Ah've seen the nicotine stains on his boxers to prove it,' says the third.

It's the sixth of November and Bridgeton is like a war-zone with all the burnt-out fireworks from the Bonfire Night. At the local primary school the teacher asks seven-year-old Jed to tell the class what he'd been caught doing the night before.

'Well miss, Ah was caught putting rockets up cats' arses,' he said.

'You mean rectum, Jed.'

'Rectum, Miss? They're fuckin' deid!'

Two little neds are hanging around the street corner, outside the Spar, when a Church of Scotland minister approaches.

'Ho! Mister! Did you no' hear? The Devil's deid!'

'In that case,' answered the minister, 'I must pray for two fatherless wee boys.'

Wee Brooklyn has made it into school for the last day of term. His teacher asks everyone to give a sentence using the word 'contagious'. Little Beyonce pipes up with, 'Ma mum was in hospital and we werenae allowed to go in tae see her because she was contagious'.

Little Britney-Lou says, 'We were at my gran's fortieth birthday party and ma step-papa said my laugh was contagious.'

The teacher said, 'Well done little Beyonce and little Britney-Lou! Those are very good examples! Now Brooklyn, what about you?'

Brooklyn stood up and launched into his story, 'We were stuck in a traffic jam and ma da said, "For fuck's sake, these road works are outrageous, by the way. See that dick digging that hole? That'll take that c**t ages."'

A primary class were having their Cycle Proficiency Test in the playground when wee Tamara knocked over two cones and skidded to a halt on the concrete. The policeman stopped the whole class and pointed out the dangers of going too fast and not paying attention and made them all realise how dangerous it could've been had it been a real accident on the road.

The policeman asked the class to tell him of a time when they'd been careless on their bikes and either fallen off or skidded and left a mark on the road. Almost everyone had a story to tell until it was the turn of Dawna who said, 'I don't have a bike of ma own but some people call ma big sister a bike and Ah heard her tell her pal that, after her boyfriend rode her on the bedroom floor, he'd left skidmarks on the carpet.'

A social worker knocks on the door of a client. A young boy around eight answers. He's smoking a cigarette and has a can of lager in his hand. The social worker is shocked and asks if his parents are at home. The kid laughs, taps his fag ash with his finger and says, 'Of course they are. Do you think Ah'd be left alone with a box of matches!'

An old lady is walking along the street and sees a boy smoking a cigarette and swigging from a beer can at a bus stop. 'Shouldn't you be at school?' she asks.

'School?' he says, 'Are you for real, auld yin? Ah'm only four.'

Pocahontas is in the Fort Shopping Centre, looking at the prams for her new baby, when her old pal Cosmo sees her and comes over for a look.

'Oh, he's pure beautiful,' she says. 'Just like his da.'

'Aye but Ah wish he was more like ma boyfriend,' says Pocahontas.

Wee Sinead is given a school project on 'Babies and Birth'. Her first question when she got home from school was, 'Ma, how was Ah born?'

'The stork brought you to us,' replied her ma.

'And how did you and ma da get born?'

'Well the stork brought us, too.'

'And what about ma granny and granda, did the stork bring them too?'

'Aye,' replied her ma, 'the stork brought us all.'

The next day Sinead went to school and told her teacher that she'd be unable to do her project on the chosen subject. The teacher seemed surprised and asked why.

'Well, there's no' been a natural birth in ma family for years, miss, so how can Ah do a project on it?'

A little boy is in the queue at Lidl with his da and he says to the woman next to him, 'You're really fat but it's cos you're having a wean, isn't it?'

The pregnant woman smiles and says that she is indeed pregnant.

'See, Ah telt you da, she is having a wean and you said her fat belly was to match her fuckin' fat arse!'

Ricky had been called in by the Job Centre and as his other half was at court that day he was forced to take wee Rick with him. As they walked along Rick said, 'Da, why is grass green?'

'Ah don't know, son.'

'Da, why is the sky blue in the day-time and black at night-time?'

'I don't know, son.'

'Da, why is dug shit different colours of brown?'

'I don't know, son.'

'Da, sorry to ask so many questions.'

'Ye're aright, wee man – if ye don't ask then you'll never learn anything.'

The nedette went to the doctor and said, 'Haw, doc. I want to have kids but no one wants to shag me and every morning, when Ah get up and look in the mirror, Ah feel like throwing up. What's wrong with me?'

And the doctor said, 'I don't know what's wrong with you but your eyesight is perfect.'

A nedette, desperate to have weans, went to the doctor. She was so depressed that she couldn't get a date that she'd swallowed a bottle of sleeping pills. The doctor told her to have a few drinks and get some rest.

Destiny, a nedette, found an S&M mag under her son, Amoruso's, bed. Upset, she showed it to the boy's dad, Dwayne. He looked at it and handed it back.

'What do you think we should do?' Destiny asked. 'Ah'm pure worried sick.'

Dwayne shrugged, 'Well, Ah wouldnae spank him, hen.'

9

Ned Moral Code
by Keanu and Beaver

See oor pal in Bar-L, Beaver, man? He's got a book deal
of his own now, man. He's been writing solidly since he
went in there and it's a best-seller now, by the way. It's all
about gangs and that. Beaver says he writes mostly from
memory, man – cop shows he saw in the nineties, man,
and stuff on telly. Rest of it he makes up.

But he gied us this code thing, man. Beaver is totally
strong – he swears by living to a code, man. Discipline is
everything, he says. Without discipline and sticking to
it, you're lost, man. He should know. He was never up
before noon in the old days and never in bed before
4 a.m. Two bottles of Buckie, one of Bru and a packet of
Cheesy Wotsits and he was ready for whatever the day
held – which was mostly jewellery shops, banks, building
societies and other people's cars, man. Hope you like
Beaver's code, by the way.

Obey the Saturday and keep it for parties, man.

Thou shalt not kill, by the way, man.

Thou shalt not be caught chibbin'.

Thou shalt not be caught stealin', ya bam.

Thou shalt run fast at the sound of a polis siren.

Thou shalt not shag yer best pal's burd.

Thou shalt have only one god – daytime telly's Trisha Goddard.

Honour thy ma and da, if you're hame before they're in bed at night.

Keep the bus stop holy.

10

Ned Crime
by Keanu

Who says crime doesn't pay? Look at oor family. None of oor parents have ever worked a day in their lives and we want for nothing! We've got everything in oor hooses. Sky movies, broadband, plasma screens, pure leather sofas, big American fridges that even make ice, a SMEG oven (it has a special fast defrost for frozen pizzas), this state-of-the-art microwave that makes the skin on roast potatoes for Christmas dinner pure golden, iPods, a digi-phone you can use when you're in the garden soaking up the rays and a moby with digicam, man. We could pay, but we don't. Some of oor gear is aquired and some is on tick. It can be a pain in the arse when you've got to avoid the bailiffs but, if they do catch us in and clear the place, we just get it replaced with newer models. Nae bother.

Everyone we knew asked their favourite poshie for a joke for this chapter, man, cos we didn't understand what it was they wanted. Then Darius keyed them all in down the pet shop in his spare time, man, between card games and feeding the python. We don't think these are funny, by the way, but one poshie called Sebastian said, 'Keanu, if people buy your book because of this chapter, then that will prove that crime does pay.' Thought he was pure funny, man. So Ah decked him.

What do you call a ned in a suit?
The accused.

What do you call five neds in a 500m sprint?
Chased.

In a courtroom, a ned was on trial. The judge asked the victim if she recognised the defendant.

'Oh, yes, your honour, that's definitely him. He's got a face only a mother could love.'

At which point the ned shouted, 'That's pure shite, man – Ah had a balaclava oan!'

Why did the ned cross the road?
Does it matter? How did he get out of prison?

Did you read about the nedette who
robbed her local Farmfoods?
She tied up the safe and
blew the cashier.

How do you know when a ned is lying?
His lips are moving.

What do you say to a nedette in
the Edinburgh marathon?
Don't bother, hen, the runners
don't carry purses.

What's the politically correct term for a
ned who hears the siren of a police car?
An athlete.

Did you hear about the nedette who filled out a Legal Aid form? Where it said 'sign here', she put Sagittarius.

Did you hear about the youngest ned in the world to go to court? To avoid being recognised, he wore his nappy over his head.

Did you hear about the six-year-old ned criminal? He followed in his parents' fingerprints.

'Aw, man, it's yer latest DAB - I'll need mair than a tenner.'

There was a recent burglary at Hearts Football Club trophy room. Police are checking the homes of all known neds in the Gorgie area for a burgundy carpet.

Did you hear about the ned who broke into the sex shop in Dalry? He got banged up.

Collette, a small nedette, went with her ma to visit her grandma's grave. On the way back, she asked her ma why some graves had two people in them.

'Whit do you mean, Collette?' her ma asked. 'They don't bury more than one in a grave.'

'I saw a grave that said, "Here lies Tommy Kilfinger, a loan shark and an honest man."'

What did the loan shark say when
asked to change a light bulb?
'I'll be back on Tuesday. You
got a problem with that?'

Why does a ned think that lawyers
should be buried twelve metres under?
Because, deep down, lawyers are OK.

What do you get if you cross a
loan shark with a lawyer?
An offer you can't understand.

What's the difference between
a loan shark and a vampire?
A vampire only sucks the blood
out of you at night.

What's the difference between
a loan shark and a gigolo?
A gigolo can only screw one person at a time.

A ned was caught shoplifting a leather bag in an expensive department store. As he was on his final warning from his parole officer, he panicked and offered to buy the bag. After consultation, the store manager agreed to sell the bag and not take the matter any further. The sale was rung through the till and the receipt presented to the ned who said, 'For fucksake, man, it's a bag no' a motor. Have you no' got anything cheaper?'

How many neds does it take to change a light bulb?
Seven – one to steal the getaway car; one to drive the getaway car; one to give the directions to get to

Drumchapel B&Q Warehouse where they sell the bulbs; one to steal the people carrier when they realise the get-away car's not big enough for them all; one to steal 40p from his ma's purse to buy the bulb; one to put the bulb in; and one to light the spliffs when they realise they dropped the bulb going up the ladder to change it.

What do you call a ned with no legs?
Anything you like, he can't chase you.

Little Oprah was telling her classmates that her dad had a new car. The teacher overheard and asked if he was excited about it. 'Yes,' said Oprah, 'ma da has spent all weekend spray painting it a different colour and swapping the number plates.'

Two thirty-five-year-old nedette grandmothers were talking on the bus about a new arrival. One says of her new grandson, 'He's gonnae be one tae watch when he's older.' Her pal asks why and she says, 'He's got his da's eyes, his ma's nose and the midwife's mobile phone.'

A ned runs up to a young couple outside a jeweller's.
   'Have you seen the polis?' shouts the ned.
   'No,' cries the young couple. 'Are you in trouble?'

The ned shouts, 'No, you are. Gie's your fuckin' wallet.'

A middle-aged woman drives up to her house in Marchmont, Edinburgh, with her Mitsubishi 4WD covered in leaves, twigs and mud. Her husband is amazed and asks where on earth she's been to get the car in that state.

'Sorry,' she says, somewhat dishevelled herself. 'I hit a ned on the way home.'

Her husband isn't too bothered. 'Well that's what the blood's about but what about all the leaves and grass?'

'I had to go off-road and chase him across the Meadows,' the woman replies.

An old man is on the waiting list for a heart transplant and gets an urgent call from the heart consultant, who informs him he has a choice of three donors. One is a young sportsman, the second is a middle-aged housewife who doesn't drink or smoke. The third is a ned. The old man says, 'I'll take the ned's heart, please.' The consultant is rather taken aback and asks why. The old man says, 'It's an easy decision to make – the ned's heart has never been used.'

A ned escapes from Barlinnie and turns up at home. His wife says, 'Where the fuck have you been? You escaped ten hours ago.'

11

A Court of Law and a Wired Jaw
by Keanu

What a pure beamer for us. How are you supposed tae hold your heid up high in the scheme when you've got family who've been caught committing crimes? Ah mean, don't get fuckin' caught. Ah was only caught the first seventy-six times, which is a pure record by the way in the UK. Caught seventy-six times in ten years, man, which is no bad considering Ah've stolen pure hunners of motors a year, man.

What happened was ma ma and ma sister, Chanelle, had gone intae the toon. Chanelle had left oor ma to meet her pals at the Trongate and do a bit of shopping but Chanelle and Toni-Lee were bagging themsel's new gear for a night oot they planned at Cleopatra's. They were spotted in New Look and followed to Internacionale and nabbed as they left there with the gear doon the front of Chanelle's Nevica ski jacket. Toni-Lee made a run for it and got away fae the store detective but in the struggle she dropped her Farmfoods bag wi' a week's dinners in it and she lost her Burberry scrunchie when the security guard grabbed her by the hair.

Being a true pal, oor Chanelle wasnae going tae dob in her mate so she got charged and was released on bail to appear in the court at a later date. The months pure dragged by until the day finally came. We all piled intae the Corsa and headed for the court. Ma ma was pure nervous but Chanelle kept a cool heid and was looking good. Mini-skirt, high heels, hair extensions tied up on the top of her heid and a crop top wi' hunners of gold chains and she'd even gone on the sunbeds every day for a week to look nice and orange.

When we were sitting waiting aboot tae be called, we saw a few neighbours and folk we knew and that. They'd been huckled in by the polis too, so we didnae feel as bad. In fact we all decided tae have a party on giro day tae cheer oorsel's up. Just then, who appeared but that burd I'd been seeing, Donna-Marie. Ah know she's used goods, cos she's been with Skid, but she's a top shag, man. Ah didnae know, but she was in as a character witness for her brother who was accused of a double murder. Pillar of the community and that, she's a top burd.

We got chatting and she invited me to a party that night so that was me sorted for later. Ah agreed tae meet her at nine in the bar, man, and that we'd get a taxi to this flat. Everything was sorted but, next thing Ah felt a whack tae ma coupon and there was blood pouring fae ma mooth. One of the family of the murder victim that her brother was accused of killing had waded intae me. Pure animal, man. The guards and polis pulled him aff me but he'd totally broke ma jaw, man. So we were on oor way to the Royal Infirmary, again, man, and the sauce was dripping down me and the nurses took me straight through.

The doctor took a look and said, 'All I can do is wire it up.' Ma jaw, man. And Ah said, 'Haw, man, not my jaw, man.' And he said, 'It'll only be for two weeks. You can eat through a straw.' The painkillers he gave me were pure mental – Ah couldnae feel a thing and Ah asked that wee burd of a nurse oot again, man. Ah can tell she was pure up for it.

So Ah was all wired, man, and she was coming on to me and Ah said, 'Well, Ah can still shag ya with this thing on, man.' She pulled me through a door and we were in a cupboard. It was full of towels. You see that stuff on *ER* and *Casualty* all. The time so they must all be at it, man, they doctors and nurses, man. Pure shaggers with all they degrees and all. Is a towel cupboard the best they brain boxes can come up with, man? They can stitch me up and gie me brain surgery but they cannae sort out a decent room for shagging. Why don't they convert a few rooms and make them like the Royal Hilton Infirmary, man, and then the docs and nurses can have their luxury rather than being shoved up against some bald towels with NHS written in fuck-off letters all over them.

Anyway, man, who wants one of they towels used for shagging? That hospital virus bug thing must have a field day on them. Never mind the cleaners – those doctors and nurses don't wash their hands before going intae the towel cupboard, man. Anyway, the shag was pure radge and Ah gied her some old chat about calling her, man, but, to be honest, Ah'm not sure she could understand me as my jaw was wired together.

So Ah swaggered out of there, man, and the pain killers were just radge, man, cos Ah was still knocked for six when Donna-Marie came to the treatment room to pick me up. Ah wrote on this piece of paper, man, 'Do you have your asthma thingy with you?' cos Ah didn't want her ill and collapsing on me again. Ah didnae want to have to go back to the hospital wi' her and run the risk of walking intae towel-cupboard burd. Mind you, man, we'd probably have had time for another round while Donna-Marie was getting treated. Ah'm a fast worker, if you know what Ah mean.

Anyway, Donna-Marie said she did have her asthma thingy wi' her and, pure bless, man, she had a packet of straws for me that she bought at the hospital shop while Ah was up that wee nurse.

It was getting late and Ah wondered how Chanelle had got oan. But ma ma and da would've phoned if anything bad had happened so we went straight tae the pub, man, and Ah had two pints of cider through that straw and she just had hauf a pint of cider cos she had the motor, man. So then Ah had a pint of voddie and tomato juice, just to get in the mood (Ah had my own bottle with me, man, and we topped up the pint under the table) and she had a few shots too. It was all getting loud and raucous, man, considering she was doing all the talking and Ah could only nod and make my noises like 'haw' and 'aw' and 'nnn'. She did ask me what was different to normal but Ah think she was just making a joke, like, man.

So then we went to this flat in Sighthill and to the party and Ah was drinking voddie from the bottle by this time, man, and, by the time we got to the room with the dancing, the walls were pure spinning, man. And Ah thought, 'Aw, naw, man, Ah'm gonnae boak.' But Ah couldn't warn anyone and it all came up in my mouth, man, and it was pure disgusting as it couldn't get through my teeth, what with the wire. Or so Ah thought, so Ah tried to swallow it but that made it worse and then up it came again, man, but tons more this time and with carrots, pounds of them, knocking against my teeth. George Lucas had nothing on what happened next, man. The vomit came pure gushing out across the room through the gaps in ma teeth. Ah suppose there are quite a few gaps, thinking back on it now. And out it came, pouring pure pints of it, spraying across the room, man, across all those radge dancers. And everyone's going, 'Oh, man!' and some people threw up as well, man, there on the spot – it was pure disgusting.

Then Ah tried to get control of masel' and some people were running, man, – it was like a disaster movie. So this laminate floor, man, it was pure stinking and so was Ah, man, and the rest of the people at the party and in walked Donna-Marie and she brought me a drink and for a drink hersel' and she said, 'Whit the fuck's that smell?' Well, Ah took a look at her, man, and I had tae run tae the window as it was pure vomit-strewn in there, man, and revolting. And Ah lost more out the windae.

She said she'd take me hame, man. Everyone was looking at her like she was pure mental, man. Ah still reckon

Ah'm a pure catch, man. It's no' every day you have tae get your jaw wired and these things happen, man. All these dobbers are just too tense. They need tae lighten up.

Donna-Marie dropped me off and ma ma started greeting when she saw the state of ma face. It was all cut, bruised and swollen and Ah suppose the spew made it look mental too. To make matters worse, after Ah went to casualty, oor Chanelle's case was called and she was jailed for ten months. She didnae help hersel' by calling the judge 'a prick' and 'a pure bawbag' but they took her previous record intae account as well.

Ma da was OK aboot it cos he's been inside anyway but ma ma was gutted. Wi' me, they got used to the court cases and stuff but ma ma wondered how any daughter of hers could bring the shame of being caught by the polis oan the family. She was concerned about oor reputation in the scheme and how everyone would think we were soft as shite – quite right, too. Ah took a pure slagging fae ma mates and that drive up tae Stirling can be a bastard in the winter. But you learn by yer mistakes and Ah'm sure she'll no' be so stupid again. Next time she better run faster and no' take Toni-Lee wi' her.

And what's the world coming tae when you can't even hang aboot in the court, minding your own business, without being attacked? Oor Chanelle was shitting hersel' as it was, not knowing what sort of sentence to expect and that. Just as well Donna-Marie was there for me. She's a pure saint, that wummin. She kept me going through the whole ordeal and made me realise that Ah'm pure dead lucky and that loads of people would love to have the family and life that Ah have. And know what? She's right. Pure spot-on!

Ah've got loads of family around me, hundreds of relations, never short of money, mates to hang aboot with, a motor, a burd that loves me and pure designer claes and sportswear that others would love to h.. Some of ma mates are jealous of ma claes and Ah can tell that their burds think Ah'm a pure catch and a brilliant ride and that. Aye, sometimes things are hard but it's no' bad being Keanu really.

12

Ned Health
by Keanu's mate Crash

My brother Bern died in pure tragic circumstances, man and he'd just had his false teeth fitted the week before and looked pure sorted. For years he'd had rotten stumps and big gaps in his mouth but, after his burd left him – when his abscess burst into her mouth when they were snogging and she went pure mental – he decided tae go and get false teeth.

He went tae a dentist and got a pair of pure white dentures. We did piss ourselves laughing at first cos he looked like a racehorse but we got used to it. His burd called him Shergar, man. He was a pure handsome hunk with his new teeth. Ah don't know why the burd was so put out by the pus from the abscess. She was minging, anyway. She had a fight wound from a cat-fight. She got chibbed in a fight with her ma and had to have 266 stitches. And she had that alcohol poisoning, man, when she was eleven. She was always a bit slow on the uptake after her carbon monoxide poisoning, although oor ma said she'd never been right cos of the drugs.

Jade, the burd, got 300 hours community service for possession of temazapam and other stuff. Her prosecution said she wasn't an abuser of drugs, just a user. Bern used to say she just uses three times a day, every day. After the court case, she went into rehab and Bern pure looked after that wean. He gave up a lot to be a good father, man, and all he got was pure criticism cos he became a father at the age of thirteen but he was younger than Jade. Everyone said Jade was a pure late developer cos she didn't have a wean till she was eighteen when wee Amber was born.

My brother Bern was pure totally devoted tae his family, man, when he was taken fae us. He doted on the wean and that and he'd probably have even forgiven Jade for being a bit shitty when the abscess burst and would've taken her back. That was all Bern wanted – a burd and a wean. Now that he's gone, we've asked them to move in with us. The family allowance and her incapacity benefit will come in handy. We're no' daft in this hoose, no way, by the way.

Bern was a pure funny guy – life and soul of every party and liked a laugh. All his mates have been round for a get-together and we remembered the good times. Ma ma was pure greeting the whole night but she put on a brave face when she sang 'Chirpy, Chirpy, Cheep, Cheep' on the karaoke – it was one of Bern's favourites. Here's a few of his mates' jokes that kept us going that night. Bern would have laughed, too, especially if he thought Kylie was buying silicone with the profits.

What happens when a nedette gets Alzheimer's?
Her IQ goes up.

The ned's family were so poor that, when the social worker went to visit and stepped on a cigarette butt, the ned ma asked, 'Who turned off the heating?'

How do you change a ned's mind?
Blow in his ear.

How do you know that Buckie and Tennents
are good for your eyesight?
Have you ever seen a ned wearing glasses?

A ned walks into his doctor's surgery and waits his turn to speak to the receptionist. 'Ah've got a problem wi' me prick,' he says.

The receptionist is appalled and tells him to say he has something wrong with another part of his anatomy because there are children present and asks him to refrain from using such language.

The ned is really annoyed by this but, managing to contain his rage, he says, 'Ah've a problem with ma nose – you see, Ah cannae pish oot it.'

A ned walked into a chemist to buy a deoderant.
'Ball or aerosol?' asked the chemist.
'It's for ma pits, man, not my baws.'

What do the government's five portions
a day mean to a ned?
Crisps, frozen pizzas with chips,
fags and Buckie.

What's the difference between a
real man and a ned?
A ned doesn't even know what a quiche is.

A ned wakes up in hospital and is surrounded by doctors.

'What's the script doctor? Why am Ah here?'

'You've had an accident involving a quad bike. Now there is some good news but also some bad.'

'Aw, gie's the bad first, doctor,' the ned said.

'Both your legs have been amputated but the good news is that your new trainers and trackie bottoms will fit the guy in the next bed.'

A nedette is lying on a stretcher in a hospital corridor after a cat-fight over a man in her local. She's naked apart from the sheet that covers her but a man in a white coat comes along, lifts the sheet, has a look at her and goes away. This happens several times until she eventually asks when she will be admitted to a ward.

'Oh, Ah don't know, hen,' the man replies, 'Ah'm the maintenance man, no' a doctor.'

Tiffany went to the doctor with bad knee pain but, after running numerous tests, the doctor couldn't find anything wrong. He called her back the following week and asked if there was anything she could think of that could be causing the problem.

'Aye, well, it's probably cos Barry and me shag doggy style every night, doctor.'

'I see,' said the doctor. 'You do know there are lots of other positions to have sex in. Perhaps a book might help?'

'Aye, Ah know that, doctor, but at least this way we can both see the telly.'

A nedette is lying in her hospital bed recovering after being operated on. The doctor on his rounds stops at her bed and is reading her notes when she asks how long she should wait before having sex.

He replied, 'I'm not really sure, I've never been asked that after removing a patient's tonsils.'

What does a ned think is a balanced diet?
A burger in each hand.

A nedette goes to the doctor with a sore throat and the doctor says her tonsils will have to be removed. She becomes abusive and demands a second opinion.

The doctor says, 'OK, your tonsils will have to be removed, you are a drain on society and you're a dog into the bargain.'

What does a ned have for a seven-course dinner?
A six pack of super lager and a KFC.

What do you give the nedette
who has everything?
Penicillin.

What's the difference between a
twelve-year-old nedette
and a twenty-five-year-old nedette?
A generation.

How is a ned like a laxative?
They both irritate the shit out of you.

A rather overweight ned, Grant, went to the doctor concerned about his ballooning weight. The doctor prescribed a new miracle diet pill where the patient puts it up their bum and comes back after a week. Grant comes back after a week, three stones lighter but bent double. The doctor says the difference is amazing but notices that Grant has a postural problem and asks if he's followed the instructions correctly. Grant replies that he has been taking the tablets but he has had some difficulty with the nil-by-mouth part – the frozen pizza was difficult to get up but that chewing gum was a nightmare.

Depressed, a ned makes an appointment to see his GP.

'Doctor, Ah cannae sleep, man,' he says.

'Have you tried counting sheep?' asks the doctor.

'Aye, man, but Ah'm still awake when Ah get tae fourteen and Ah don't know whit tae dae next.'

Did you hear about the ned who was
bitten by a pit bull?
The ned was fine but the pit bull
died of alcohol poisoning.

A ned was lying in hospital with his face fully bandaged having been attacked by a Rottweiler and a rat. A very pretty nurse called Cecilia approached him, 'Is there anything you need?'

His voice from behind the bandages was muffled and he mumbled several phrases involving the word 'testicles'. The nurse duly obliged and reached under the sheet to examine him.

'You know,' she said sweetly, 'Everything seems to be in order down there. Is there anything else I can do for you?'

The ned nodded and from behind the bandages mumbled another phrase which again involved the word 'testicles'. The nurse smiled sweetly again and put her head and hands under the sheet and examined, at length, his testicles.

She surfaced and sighed, 'Everything under there is just perfect.'

At this point, the ned, ripped the bandage away from his mouth. 'Haw, doll!' he cried. 'Take your hands aff ma baws! Ah was asking you if ma test results are back and are they OK?'

A ned, who was high on drugs, went into the health centre and asked to see the doctor. The nurse took him straight through.

'What seems to be the problem?' said the doctor.

'Haw, doctor, Ah'm pure tripping and Ah think Ah'm a moth, man.'

The doctor examines him and tells the ned that he is indeed hallucinating but that he isn't a moth. 'Why did you come in?' the doctor asks.

'Haw, doc, Ah saw the light on.'

13

Ned Fashion
by Kylie

See me? Ah'm pure over the moon. Ah'm wearing ma New Look trackie top and the bling-bling rings ma last three men got me and no one here can believe Ah'm a 36D without implants. It's all me, man, up top and out front. A lot of girls are pure flat-chested and Ah feel pure sorry for them, by the way, as it's great to be decked out like a pure woman. A man likes that.

Ah was a size twelve but Ah slimmed down to a pure size ten. Ah went to a diet centre in Edinburgh, man, and it was pure dead posh. It cost me eighty quid a week on diet pills. It was pure willpower and speed tablets, man, Ah was high and starving for three months. You could eat anything that you wanted – but crisps and chocolate have done the trick for me, man.

Those celebrities are pure thin, by the way, and Ah sympathise with anyone over a size ten, like ma pal Paris Milton. She needs to drop five dress sizes, man, and had an ugly fat stomach, man, and she took these green tea capsules she bought from the internet, man – Ah think they came from America. She wants to look like JLo or Caprice. That JLo has a big arse, by the way.

Ma favourite shops for fashion are JD Sports, JJB,

AllSports and Internacionale. Britney prefers New Look but you can't pull in there cos it's all burds that work there. The lads in the sports shops are pure shagable. Keanu reckons we've got real purchasing power now and can set oor ain style, man. We have to look good when we're oot and aboot, especially for hanging round the Spar shop and bus stops. At least, that's what Darius is right into now. Ah asked Darius and he wrote down his thoughts on fashion, he's pure trendy, that boy.

First, right, you have to make sure your hair looks good. Lads have a shaved heid with tramlines and maybe blond bits at the front or they might grow it in a bit but have their fringe gelled so it shows doon the front of their baseball caps, man. Loads of the burds have a 'facelift' ponytail pulled through the back of their caps or they just have straight hair dyed blonde but mair and mair lassies are having dark roots tae show they're no' real blondes and aren't pure dafties, man.

Trackies are oor uniform wi' designer logo T-shirts. Ah paid fifty quid for ma new Mackenzie T-shirt the other week, man, and it's the dug's baws – all the burds love it too, by the way. The lassies wear the same. You can be sure tae attract a ned or nedette if you stick tae the same uniform and then ye can swap claes wi' yer burd if ye want withoot being called a poofter.

Tucking trackies intae white socks is pretty cool too, the whiter the better – only pure wee tramps would be oot in dirty white that's washed oot. White trainers complete the look. It can take some of us two weeks tae save up the ninety quid for the average pair – thank fuck for benefit fraud and cheap deals behind the local pub, man, otherwise we'd be pure scuppered.

A lot of the burds are going for fake tans or they tan stands. Some lads go but ye either have tae be pure orange or pure pasty white, man, and there's nae in between.

Right, jewellery – the mair you wear the mair money you look like you have so wear it all at once is oor advice. Sovvy rings are quality but a ring on every finger is a ned basic. Earrings are essential too, man. Loads of burds have five or six heavy gold ones in each ear – nae wonder their lobes are nearly doon at their shoulders, man.

Chains are heavy and chunky for the lads but the burds usually add a hologram pendant of a deid relative or someone in the jail. A name chain completes the look and hunners of bracelets too. Ah have tae admire some of they lassies for the weight they carry roon their necks and they walk tall and proud. Elizabeth Duke and HPJ have got the average ned likes of us tae thank for their success. So get yersel intae Trongate, take ma fashion tips seriously and get yersel some serious ned gear. Ah'm telling you, man, it's the way forward.

Kylie again:

Since Keanu and Ah have come back from America Ah reckon Ah'm going to get asked to do a style column, man. Ah read *OK*, *Hello* and *National Enquirer* to keep up to date with what's happening in the style stakes, by the way. Ah just got a black Diesel raincoat and DKNY aviator sunglasses. It was a pure bitch to get them as Ah thought this pure hunk of a security guard was gonna nab me, man, know what Ah mean?

He was a pure tomcat when Ah went down on him in the security office. He was pure tottie and eye candy for the girls. Ah was pure miffed that he didn't want to see me again and he pure sneered at me when Ah told him it was hard tae swallow but all ma mates know that Ah'm a spitter. Ah was pure pure crushed that Ah didn't get some Dior gear before he escorted me oot.

I don't care anyway cos Ah've just come out of a love triangle. Ah'm pure drop dead gorgeous and Ah'm glad Ah'm out of that as Ah got mixed up with two no marks that Ah met in the alcohol treatment centre, man. Ah was so glad to see the back of those bawbags cos now Ah can concentrate on Britney's twins and ma fashion column.

> What do you call a forty-year-old nedette
> shopping for maternity clothes?
> A pregnant granny.

How do neds sort out their laundry?
Dirty and dirty-but-it'll-do-another-few-days.

Why do nedettes have pierced belly buttons?
It gives them something to hang
the air freshener from.

What's the difference between a ned and a pit bull?
The jewellery.

Simone, a young nedette, walked into a haidresser to get her highlights and extensions done. She was wearing huge headphones and a Walkman. 'See me, Jackie?' she said. 'See ma heid? Ah need these men to get me through the day. Gonnae cut round them?'

Jackie did a double take but agreed in the end. She worked as best she could around the headphones, attaching the blonde extensions and highlighting the top of Simone's head. Simone was very pleased, admiring herself from side to side, now the black slick of old hair had been covered up.

Jackie, however, was intrigued by what Simone had been listening to for so long without changing her CD. Under the dryer she put on a very low setting so that Simone would not have an electrical blow-out on either side of her head.

Eventually, Simone nodded off and Jackie, going to check on how the black was changing to blonde under the dryer, removed the headphones to see what she was listening to. Simone suddenly slumped in her chair, dead. Jackie dialled 999 and tried to resuscitate her. The paramedics, on arrival, took her away to jump-start her into action.

Jackie the hairdresser, meanwhile, grabbed the earphones and heard, 'Inhale ... exhale ... inhale ... exhale ...'

What do you call a ned shopping for a new trackie?
Déjā vu.

What do you call a ned in the pub
with a DKNY watch and an iPod?
Stop-me-and-buy-one.

Have you seen the ads for the new shampoo for neds?
Go & Wash.

A family of neds head up to Aberdeen to see their grandparents and at the same time to see their father in Peterhead jail. The youngest, wee Michaela, falls into a river and an American tourist manages to drag her to safety but the kid is pretty shaken up. The grandparents trail round every city centre hotel and eventually find the tourist.

'Are you the yank that saved oor Michaela?' growled her granda.

'Indeed I am, sir,' replied the American, pleased as punch with himself.

'Well, you owe us ninety quid, mate. She lost wan o' her trainers when ye dragged her oot the watter and they're only weeks' old.'

Jade, a nedette, went to the tattooist for a picture of Eminem on the inside of her left thigh. The tattooist made what he thought was a similar likeness and was pleased with the result. He told Jade he was finished and invited her to look.

'That's pure vile, man. Ah cannae see whit it is!'

The tattooist was taken aback, thought it over and offered to try again on the inside of her opposite thigh.

'Aw, OK,' agreed Jade, thinking two Eminems would make her drop-dead gorgeous.

So the tattooist went to work and, when he was finished, Jade inspected the image.

'Pure shite, man,' was her judgement. 'That's no' him.'

In despair, the tattooist went into the bar next door and looked for someone who looked as though they could identify Eminem. He grabbed a chap who looked bright and who was carrying a fiddle case.

'Excuse me,' the tattooist said. 'Do you know about rap?'

'Oh, aye,' said the chap 'I used to write for *NME*.' And he then proceeded to weave his way across the bar, drunk as a stoat, and out into the street, following the tattooist.

'Can you identify which musician this is on this girl's legs, please?' the tattooist asked.

The drunk made his way across the room and peered between Jade the ned's legs, which were by now wide-open, ready for inspection. The drunk took a good long look and then announced, 'Well, Ah don't know about the other two but the one in the middle's Willie Nelson.'

14

The Ned Alphabet
by Kylie and Keanu

Everyone says we can't talk right. Well, we know oor alphabet just as well as the posh publisher guy. We're not pure illiterate, by the way. So here's a few A–Zs from oor world. Anything you don't understand? Just phone the posh guy and ask!

A is for aw, arse, Ah'm, ASBO
B is for Buckie, baws, bawbag, buroo, Burberry, beamer, bender, beaver, burd, Bar-L, bevvy, boak (as in 'It gie's me the boak, man.')
C is for c**t, caps, cum, court, cargo, chemist, chav, Cornton Vale, chippy, council, chibbed
D is for dug's baws, dobber, dick, da, doctor's waiting room, dry boak, diddies
E is for eejit, Eminem
F is for fit, flip, fitba, fake designer, fake tan, firearms, fanny, fannybaws
G is for *Grease* (the film), giro, gold jewellery, grass, gob
H is for 'Hawwww, man!', housing benefit, hummin',

hash, hoose, hangover, housing list, housing benefit, happy slap, hawmans (as in 'kicked in the hawmans')

I is for inside

J is for jacksie, jail, judge, job seeker's allowance, jakey, japs-eye

K is for Kinder Buenos, knocked-off, knob, knobbler

L is for Leith, lack of employment, lethargic, lazy, lout, Legal Aid

M is for '(Pure) Mental, man!', man, motors, ma, McDonald's

N is for naw, nappies on prescription, non-educated delinquents

O is for oor, offie

P is for pure, pregnant, polis, puke, pished, pure-pished, pasty (-faced), poof, prick, Pot Noodle

Q is for quality!

R is for Red Bull, ragin', roasted red raw (in the tanning shop), radge, ringers, result

S is for Stella, Stone Roses, souped-up, single mother, sorted, Super Noodles, shagging, 'shat it', stolen, spots, scrunchie, script (prescription), six-pack, social worker, steaming, shut-the-fuck-up, scunge, sicko, spunk bucket, scunge

T is for Tennents Super, tinnies, trackies, trainers, the toon, thug, twat, tosser, tats, *Trisha*, talent

U is for under-age sex, unemployed, underhand (dealings)

V is for vomit, voddie, verbal

W is for 'Whit?', weans, wanker, wet boak, wheels, warmer

X is for 'X box, man, got to have one of those, man?'

Y is for ya bam, ya beauty, ya dick, ya dancer, ya poofy
wee prick

Z is for 'Z-z-zeds, man, it's a hard life being a ned.'

15

Style Tips for Nedettes
by Britney

Hi, everyone, Britney here. Ma ma was asking the other night about the rules on dating and what not tae dae for us girls, now that everyone is pure obsessed with ladette behaviour and teenage pregnancy. So Paris Milton and me swapped notes and here's a quick guide for how to behave if you're a nedette.

Shag a man even though he's married cos you pure fancy him. Plus you'll never see him again anyhow.

Spend Sunday on waking, wondering where you are and who you are. Leave his flat to find a street sign so you can call a cab to get them to pick you up. And, when the taxi cab company says, 'Name?' you say, 'Ah cannae remember his but mine's Paris Milton.'

Bring your new boyfriend breakfast in bed – a Big Mac and fries at the bus stop.

When asked to pour wine at a posh dinner party, swig it pure straight from the bottle and laugh provocatively with the men in the room.

New style suit for the job interview that the job seeker's allowance paid for should be a hairnet from the chicken factory.

Your best style icon should be one of the following: Coleen McLoughlin, Jordan, Jodie Marsh, Kerry Katona, Jade Goodie.

Your ideal date ends with snogging a stranger at a taxi rank or shagging your date's son on the sofa.

Your dream-wedding scenario should be bride and groom with matching trackies for the ceremony in your best pal's living room.

To look like a nineteen-year-old nedette when you're a thirty-eight-year old gran, pure scrape back your hair in a scrunchie, get a pure hard as hell look on your knife-edged face, carry a Farmfoods bag full of Buckie bottles and wink at all the boys twenty years younger – pure classy.

To behave like a nedette on holiday, take your own teabags, sausages, biscuits and Mighty White sliced loaf.

16

Ned Limericks
as heard by Kylie, Keanu, Ron P and Limerick M

Nursery rhymes read straight out of book are pure boring. All the weans in oor family, and there are hundreds, have been sung to sleep with songs that we've pure made up ourselves at weddings and funerals and that. There's only a few here cos we're pure running out of paper now but they make us laugh. We hope you laugh too and hope you've enjoyed reading about us. You'll see lots of us oot and aboot everyday. Oor distinctive style means you can spot us nae bother at all. Next time you see one of us, wave and say hello. It might even be us – we cannae wait tae be pure famous.

C U l8r!

Kylie and Keanu

There was a young ned from Carluke
Who had a Rottweiler called Duke.
The dog he was frisky,
And liked to sup whisky,
But if he mixed it with Buckie he'd puke.

There was a nedette from Barlanark,
Who went down on men like Titanic,
From Barra to Wick,
She brought them off quick,
And went back for her chips to Carmunnock.

There was a young ned from Cathcart,
Who shagged a Morningside tart,
The bus stop was nippy,
So they made it a quickie,
And caught the sixty-nine bus to the park.

A five-year-old ned from the border,
Got an Anti-Social Behaviour Order,
For throwing a stone
At a shark with a loan,
And a nicked defunct camcorder.

There was a young ned from Braemar,
Who liked to drink beer from a jar,
He ordered up twenty
And when they were empty,
Said, 'Ah hope the lavvy's nae far.'

A horny nedette called Lil
Fucked a dynamite stick for a thrill
They found her vagina
In South Carolina
And bits of her tits in Harthill.

There was a nedette vampire Mabel,
Whose period was remarkably stable.
So one night in June,
She got a big spoon
And drank herself under the table.

A Scots ned Jamie MacMartin,
A bean-eating challenge took part in.
Thirty tins was enough,
He was feeling quite stuffed
And started to fart in his tartan.